The World Crisis in
Social Security

THE WORLD CRISIS IN

SOCIAL SECURITY

Jean-Jacques Rosa, *Editor*

Onorato Castellino

A. Lawrence Chickering

Richard Hemming

Martin C. Janssen

Karl Heinz Jüttemeier

John A. Kay

Heinz H. Müller

Hans-Georg Petersen

Sherwin Rosen

Ingemar Ståhl

Noriyuki Takayama

A joint project of the
Fondation Nationale d'Economie Politique,
based in Paris, and the Institute for Contemporary Studies,
based in San Francisco, California

Inquiries, book orders, and catalog requests should be addressed to
the Institute for Contemporary Studies, Suite 811, 260 California
Street, San Francisco, California 94111——415—398—3010.

ISBN 0-917616-44-8 (USA)
ISBN 2-86590-001-0 (France)

CONTENTS

vi

CONTRIBUTORS

ONORATO CASTELLINO
Professor of economics, Instituto di Economia Politica,
University of Turin, Italy

A. LAWRENCE CHICKERING
Executive director, Institute for Contemporary Studies,
San Francisco, United States

RICHARD HEMMING
Senior research officer, Institute for Fiscal Studies, London, England

MARTIN C. JANSSEN
Senior research fellow, University of Zurich, Switzerland

KARL HEINZ JÜTTEMEIER
Research fellow in public finance, Kiel Institute of World Economics,
West Germany

JOHN A. KAY
Research director, Institute for Fiscal Studies, London, England

HEINZ H. MÜLLER
Research associate, Institute for Empirical Research in Economics,
University of Zurich, Switzerland

HANS-GEORG PETERSEN
Professor of political science, University of Kiel,
West Germany

JEAN-JACQUES ROSA
Professor of economics, Institut d'Etudes Politiques de Paris, France

SHERWIN ROSEN
Professor of economics, University of Chicago, Illinois, United States

INGEMAR STÅHL
Professor of economics, Lunds Universitet, Lund, Sweden

NORIYUKI TAKAYAMA
Associate professor of economics,
Hitotsubashi University, Tokyo, Japan

PREFACE

In the last half of the 1970s, declining economic growth and continuing low fertility rates signaled the coming of a severe crisis in the financing of public retirement programs sometime after the turn of the twenty-first century. This long-run funding crisis for the first time began to overshadow short-term financing problems and the growing sense that these programs had serious inequities built into many of them. The increased concern about social security marked a dramatic turn of mind toward what had been regarded as the most successful and popular of all the programs associated with the growth of the welfare state at the end of the last century.

The funding problem is particularly important since social security programs account for a very large share of the public budgets in most industrial countries. A rethinking was thus not only advisable but even critical in order to plan for a lean national future while protecting the income security of the elderly.

Although the general problems are surprisingly similar in most industrial countries, there are important differences in both problems and remedies. This book represents an effort to bring together in one volume the experiences of eight industrial countries in a comparative analysis which might reveal solutions and lessons for policymakers grappling with these problems in each of the countries and elsewhere.

The project began with a conference, jointly sponsored by the Fondation Nationale d'Economie Politique and the Institute for Contemporary Studies and held in Paris on 15-16 October 1980. The most difficult part of any comparative study, particularly one involving multiple authors, lies in finding comparative data that reflect measurements of similar things. Since each country measures its own programs differently, it was particularly difficult to find good data to set with confidence next to data from another country. Much of the conference was spent on this problem and on assuring that each writer wrote on the same general problems in his country. In fact, the problem of reliable numbers would have been greater had the numbers been closer together.

The idea for this book was thought partly to be a natural sequel to the 1977 study of the United States' system, *The Crisis in Social Security*, edited by Michael J. Boskin. Each of the contributors to this new book is a recognized authority on social security in his own country, but only one—Sherwin Rosen—is a holdover from the earlier book.

This study represents the first collaboration of FNEP and ICS in a joint project. We hope that the results may contribute to the solution of this very great problem in many parts of the world.

A. Lawrence Chickering
Executive Director
Institute for Contemporary Studies

Jean-Jacques Rosa
President
Fondation Nationale d'Economie Politique

Paris, France
April 1982

GLOSSARY

Actuarial elements. Elements relative to statistical calculations, used particularly to establish insurance premiums.

Adverse incentives. Incentives created by social security which lead to adverse economic behavior, such as withdrawal from the labor force or reductions in private saving.

Annuity. A form of private insurance payable at specified intervals, similar to a private pension.

Autonomous programs. Retirement plans operated by self-governing organizations, generally using government funds.

Beneficiaries. Those who receive payments or benefits from particular programs—in this case, from social security systems.

Benefits. Payments or services provided under certain entitlements by a social welfare plan, annuity, pension system, or insurance policy.

Ceiling. Upper limit (1) on earnings allowed without pension deductions; (2) on salary beyond which no payroll tax is levied (as in France); and (3) on benefits allowed by social security plans.

Complementary/supplementary retirement programs. Specialized government or private pension systems which add to the benefits provided by general (basic government) social security plans.

Contracting out. Contract agreement to renounce entitlement to all or part of public insurance benefits in exchange for reduced payroll tax and the purchase of private insurance (as in the United Kingdom).

Contribution period. Minimum length of time during which contributions must be paid to establish eligibility for benefits.

CPI (consumer price index). Measure of the change in cost of goods and services in relation to their cost in some base period.

Deficit financing. Use of public funds which have been raised by borrowing rather than by taxation.

Demographics. Studies of changes in the population concerning its size, structure, density, expansion, or decline.

Dependency ratio. Ratio of workers to retirees.

Disincentives. Social security measures which deter beneficiaries from economic or other activities (see *adverse incentives*).

Disposable income. Income left after taxes.

Dissaving. To use savings for current expenses, especially during retirement.

Earmarked financing. Taxes designated to fund one specific program, such as payroll taxes to fund social security.

Earned entitlements. Benefits received according to the record of taxes paid.

Earnings-related benefits. Pensions and contributions determined as a percentage of earnings, often up to a specified ceiling.

Econometrics. Use of statistical methods in the study of economics.

Explicit debt. Taxes or bonds whose amount, maturity, and interest rate are specified when imposed or issued.

Funded system. Retirement system in which accumulated savings are invested to provide future retirement income.

GDP (gross domestic product). Differs from GNP (see below) in that GDP equals GNP less overseas income earned by citizens of that country, plus income earned within that country by citizens of outside countries.

General revenue financing. Opposed to earmarked financing; funding a government program out of funds raised by such means as income taxes.

GNP (gross national product). Total value of goods and services produced by a nation during a specified period (usually a year), including moneys earned by its citizens or businesses located abroad.

Government subsidy. A government's financial grant to an agency or private organization to assist a particular project.

Implicit debt. The indeterminate amount to be paid by future generations in order to meet the benefit claims of retirees who have paid social security contributions throughout their working lives. Neither the maturity nor the resultant return on this amount are known.

Indexation. Changes in the nominal dollar amount or a tax or benefit according to the evolution of a cost of living index.

Inflation. Sustained increase in the general price level.

Internal rate of return. Rate of return that equalizes a flow of future benefits or earnings and the present investment or disbursement.

Labor mobility. An individual's shift between jobs, either vertically (within a company) or laterally (between companies or geographical areas).

Life cycle. Stages through which an individual passes during its lifetime; in economics, with respect to income, consumption, and spending.

Mandatory programs. Programs, such as social security, in which employers and employees are required by law to participate.

Marginal productivity (labor/capital). Increment of output when one unit of labor (capital) is added.

Means testing. Determination of the amount of a contribution/benefit according to the earnings or income of the contributor/beneficiary.

Negative interest rate. Minus percentage (inferior to zero).

NNI (net national income per capita). The sum of all personal incomes within a nation.

Noncontributory programs. Income transfer programs into which beneficiaries do not pay in order to obtain entitlements.

Occupational pensions. Benefits provided to a retiree by the industry or firm for which he worked or the union to which he belonged.

Pay-as-you-go system. A system in which benefits to present nonworking beneficiaries are paid out of present taxes on working contributors.

Payroll tax. Tax deducted from an individual's pay by the employer.

Private insurance. Retirement, health, or other insurance purchased from a private commercial insurance company.

Public securities. Government bonds or treasury bills are examples.

Regressive transfers. Income transferred from the poor to give to the rich.

Replacement income/ratio. Average benefits relative to average salary.

Revaluation. Changing costs, prices, salaries, and benefits according to decreases in the value of money—inflation.

Risk capital. Capital (as retained corporate earnings or new equity) invested in enterprises as the ownership element. It guarantees the creditors of the firm in case of bankruptcy.

Self-employment income. Income earned directly from one's own business, trade, or profession rather than from an employer.

Social overhead capital. Accumulated funds invested in projects used by the general public, such as bridges, highways, etc.

Stagflation. The combination of zero growth or recession with inflation.

Standard of living. What the income can buy.

Statutory programs. Programs enacted, created, or regulated by law.

Survivor's pension. The pension granted by law to a dependent surviving a beneficiary of social security programs.

Tax base. The amount of income or capital on which the tax is calculated.

Transfer payments. Welfare payments or pensions received by individuals or families which are not compensation for produced goods or services.

Trust fund. Money or securities held in trust to produce income which is to be paid to the beneficiary at a specified date.

Underground economy. Black market or profit-making activities designed to avoid government taxation and regulation.

Unemployment dole. Government benefits granted to the unemployed.

Value-added tax (VAT). An internal tax levied incrementally on the value added at each stage of processing a raw material or producing and distributing a commodity or service.

Work/earnings test. Social security requirement which lowers a beneficiary's pension in a specified ratio to the amount of his earnings.

1

JEAN-JACQUES ROSA

Social Security and the Future

Loss of public confidence in social security. Origins and development of systems discussed. Present importance of social security. Diversity among countries. Common characteristics. What are the problems? The value of international comparison.

1

In recent years a significant change has affected public attitudes toward mandatory social security systems. Criticism of their side effects on the economy and their inequities, plus fears for their long-term viability have replaced praise for social insurance as the greatest social triumph of the second half of this century. While contributors are protesting against increases in the payroll tax, the insured wonder whether they will have a sufficient income when they retire.

Public retirement programs are important both to individuals and to national economies. They are the principal source of income for the aged in most industrial countries; in terms of dollar volume, they are the largest transfer programs in national budgets. They also operate on payroll deductions which create funds often almost as large as the operating budgets of national governments.

EVOLUTION OF THE SYSTEMS

European social security systems date back more than a century. They were created in response to the demands of rapid industrialization, when financial markets were relatively undeveloped and individuals were relatively ill informed. In societies that were primarily rural, the extended family had guaranteed an income in old age. But with industrialization and urbanization, the family framework narrowed, and it was necessary to find an alternative. Individual saving was not a reliable solution, given the poorly developed financial markets and the small number of financial institutions. Furthermore, individuals did not have the information or competence to make sound long-term financial decisions. Under these conditions there was a great risk that the improvident or the unlucky would end up an the taxpayers' charge, since common humanity required the better off to help the needy. The first workers' retirement funds were thus intended to reduce the risks of personal savings management on a firm or industry basis.

Only recently, during the 1930s and 1940s, have social security programs begun to include the majority of salaried people. And only during the 1950s and 1960s have they grown to cover almost everyone and to be based on pay-as-you-go financing rather than on actuarial funding. Yet despite these similarities, the evolution of mandatory, public, pay-as-you-go social security encompassing nearly everyone has varied in important respects from one country to another.

Retirement systems contain three elements: (1) a basic, mandatory public system; (2) complementary systems—some mandatory, some not—organized within a firm or an industry or nationally; and (3) voluntary individual insurance contracts. The role of each of these elements and the organization of the first two differ considerably between countries.

Japan is an exception to these generalizations, as Noriyuki Takayama shows, for the first two elements—the basic public program paying a flat-rate minimum benefit and a supplementary pension based on contributions, both mandatory— continue to function principally on an actuarial basis. However, the negative real return on these funds, which by law must be placed in public instruments, requires partial recourse to pay-as-you-go funding.

All other basic pension systems are financed on a pay-as-you-go basis, with variations in the financing of supplementary programs. Italy, the United States, and West Germany have no public supplementary programs but only private pensions and saving, funded actuarially. Switzerland currently has a voluntary supplementary program which is actuarially funded; but this program is being reformed to a mandatory system which will probably contain pay-as-you-go elements. Great Britain allows pensioners to opt out of its public supplementary program. Ninety percent of those eligible for this option elect to take it, and many of those substitute funded private schemes for the pay-as-you-go public system. Sweden formally has a pay-as-you-go supplementary system, but it is combined with a forced saving program which has accumulated a capital fund that is very large in relation to the Swedish capital stock. Finally, France has a pay-as-you-go supplementary program.

There are also differences in methods of calculating pensions, paying contributions, and determining the relevant tax base. Most systems supplement revenues from payroll taxes with transfers from general revenues ranging up to 20 percent of program costs (for Japan). Only France, Sweden, and the United States rely entirely on the payroll tax. Given the varying degrees of homogenization and centralization of retirement systems, the transition from one employment to another may or may not mean a loss of pension rights. One must also note that public welfare benefits such as "free" health care have recently been added to these three retirement system elements; particularly in Sweden, the elderly receive a whole host of other benefits, such as housing allowances, as well.

Because of their complexity and the differences in their structure, it is difficult to compare these eight systems. Given this diversity, it is not surprising that pensions represent significantly different fractions of gross national product, ranging from Japan's 3.67 percent in 1978 to Sweden's more than 14 percent (including medical benefits) in 1979. However, most systems pay in the range of 10 to 12 percent.

Another common element is the recourse to pay-as-you-go financing. In an actuarially sound, funded system, each worker puts aside savings during his active years for consumption after retirement, thus accumulating individual capital; but in a pay-as-you-go system, contributions deducted from active workers' salaries are immediately paid out to retirees. Employees, in paying their contributions, acquire a moral credit with future generations which they hope will, in turn, pay them pensions when they retire. But that commitment is not precise or explicit. Another difference between the two systems is that actuarial funding involves actual accumulation of savings invested in well-defined assets, whereas pay-as-you-go involves only an imprecise moral claim on the labor incomes of future generations. This difference also has important implications for the saving rates and thus for the expected economic growth in the countries studied.

RISKS AND PROBLEMS

It should be noted that the two mechanisms for financing social security entail different risks and perspectives. In a funded system, the lot of retirees depends on the real rate of return on capital. In a pay-as-you-go system, on the other hand, retiree benefits do not depend directly on real returns on capital, but on the evolution of labor incomes, demographic structures, labor force participation rates, and retirement ages. Changing circumstances could prove favorable to funded or pay-as-you-go systems, in turn.

The reasons why pay-as-you-go has been adopted in practically all of the basic programs are easy to understand. First, the funds previously accumulated by pension programs often were wiped out in the interwar or immediate postwar periods by highly variable and unanticipated inflation because governments required them to be invested in public bonds. In trying to profit from a cheap source of financing and in preventing portfolio diversification, governments dramatically increase their programs' vulnerability to inflation.

Second, economic conditions following the war were particularly favorable to pay-as-you-go; the unexpected growth in national incomes and the declining median ages of the populations allowed active workers to think that their claim on the labor incomes of future generations was secure. On the other hand, the introductory phase of a pay-as-you-go system is highly advantageous, since pensions can be paid immediately—even to the first wave, who have contributed nothing. Under these conditions, the political pressures for extending the system are strong, and this is what happened during the 1950s and 1960s. The system grew, not because it was especially well managed, but because the "chain-letter" effect brought a windfall and euphoria in the initial phase to which economic and demographic circumstances lent themselves. All of this translated into a very favorable ratio of contributors to pensioners, which made the system popular.

But the system was not free from problems. Because of its very size and rapid growth, it could not avoid inconsistencies and inequities. Its effects on savings and on the labor supply, moreover, raised concern about its impact on economic growth rates. Finally, with an aging population, its long-term financial viability is now seriously in doubt if current trends toward higher benefits are not checked.

The extreme case of administrative complexity and multiplication of specific programs is presented by Great Britain, while Italy constitutes a polar example of the permissiveness and confusion—not to mention financial stress—to which excessively easy financing can lead. But some random and hardly equitable redistributions exist in all the countries. In such large programs, which can mandate large contributions of household income, losses of supervision and control are inevitable.

There are other important side effects, principally affecting savings formation and capital accumulation, productivity, and growth. If the current generation's moral claim on future generations is perceived as secure, in buying future security contributions become equivalent to individual savings. An increase in contribution rates thus should decrease individual savings by the same amount. Since contributions are immediately distributed to retirees, there is no accumulated fund, and overall savings would therefore decrease with each contribution increase.

Retirement decisions are also affected by the level of social security pensions as well as by such conditions as the earnings test, which in some countries reduces pension benefits when retirees work for pay. While the earnings test may induce earlier retirement for certain pensioners, some of those may save more during their working lives to provide for their resulting longer period of retirement. The saving and employment effects are major concerns in all industrial countries, but their implications vary with different program settings.

THE FUTURE

At present, the major worry is the nature of the moral claim which current generations of workers possess against succeeding generations. The initial phase has already passed, and all these systems have attained maturity. All workers are contributing, and there no longer are any windfalls. At the same time, populations are aging in all advanced industrial countries, and prospects for future economic growth appear less bright than in the postwar "miracle years." The pay-as-you-go systems face medium-range projections of more retirees and fewer young workers, with incomes rising less rapidly than they did during the 1950s and 1960s. Under these conditions, the ratio of expected pensions to actual contributions is clearly falling for those now entering the work force in relation to those already receiving pensions or about to receive them. Moreover, we see no reason why the situation should stabilize or improve by the end of the century—just the opposite, in fact, unless present trends change.

The problems considered in this book are aggravated substantially by the political obstacles to serious reform. Apart from some issues of equity, the major difficulties in these programs do not have conspicuous symptoms presently associated with them. Problems of growth, and especially of long-term finance, involve consequences largely in the *future*. The present consequences tend to be relatively minor, and it is therefore difficult for politicians, whose time horizons are frequently limited to the next election, to enact meaningful reforms that impose current burdens on highly visible constituencies. At the same time, the longer the delay in reform, the greater the changes must be and the higher the resulting economic and political cost.

The political obstacles to reform make it critical that policymakers understand both the current and future problems of their countries' social security programs and the full range of options for reform. In this respect, an international perspective is especially important today, since the diversity of situations and institutions among countries reveals particular difficulties and remedies that could be useful in devising solutions. The chapters that follow provide a broader base of information for evaluating recent experience and highlighting opportunities for reform.

2

JEAN-JACQUES ROSA

France

The CNAV and supplementary retirement programs. Taxes, contributions, and indexation. Future participation rates. Intergenerational transfers and the rate of return. Impact on the national economy. Redistributional effects. Funding and pay-as-you-go.

The French social security system features a basic, mandatory program (the Caisse nationale d'assurance vieillesse—CNAV) covering all salaried workers in private industry and commerce; there are also special programs for selected groups such as farmers, tradesmen, self-employed craftsmen, civil servants, and employees of nationalized industries. These basic programs have been increasingly supplemented by complementary programs negotiated privately between employers' organizations and unions. Finally, the state also guarantees a minimum annual income of 17,000 francs (about $2,975 U.S. at the exchange rate as of 1 July 1981 [F = $0.175 U.S.]) for the elderly (aged 65 and older), regardless of participation in specific pension programs. Altogether, benefits for all forms of social retirement insurance equaled about 7.65 percent of the French gross national product (GNP) in 1979.

The basic program is a pay-as-you-go system financed by a payroll tax of 12.9 percent (8.2 percent on the employer and 4.7 percent on the employee) levied on a regulated minimum up to a 1980 ceiling of F 60,120 (worth $10,521 in 1981). Pensions in the basic program depend on the salary received during the ten best years of working life, the number of contributing years, and the retirement age, which may be any time after the age of 60. Although benefits are not formally indexed to inflation, informal indexation has evolved by legislative discretion.

The French social security system was a great success story from its founding in 1945 until 1975. In recent years, however, population aging combined with reduced economic growth have forced significant payroll tax increases to maintain benefits, and concern has arisen about the system's overall viability. Over the last three decades, in fact, contributions as a percentage of national income rose from 2.9 percent in 1950 to 9.0 percent in 1980.

This period was generally very good for pensioners because pay-as-you-go financing, in the early years of the program, implied a gift to the first generations of retirees who contributed little or nothing during their active years. The recent financing problems have hit different programs in various ways, but government efforts to find solutions by transferring funds from richer to poorer programs have come up against serious political challenges.

The pay-as-you-go system will be headed for further trouble over the longer run; the start-up advantages disappear when everyone contributes for the full number of contribution years. Population aging alone is already having a substantial effect, as the overall ratio of 4.62 workers per retiree enjoyed in 1950 declined to 2.66 in 1975, and this decline will continue to an estimated 1.76 in 2030. That, combined with declining economic growth, will severely strain the system sometime after the turn of the century. When nearly everyone has been enrolled in the system, as is now the case, this problem can be solved only by substantial increases in the payroll tax, with corresponding harmful effects on incentives to work and save, or by reductions in the replacement rate, which set pensions equal to 41.9 percent of last wages in 1980. In either event, the apparent rate of return on contributions will decline progressively in future years.

The effects of social security on saving involve counteracting influences. On the one hand, although no actual saving occurs in a pay-as-you-go system, the transfer of purchasing power from working to retirement years has the same effect as personal savings; increasing payroll taxes therefore will tend to reduce private saving. On the other hand, earlier retirement encourages increased saving to provide for a longer retirement period. Attempts to verify net saving effects in France are still unresolved.

Unlike other countries, France does not have an earnings test. Retirees gain pensions as of right whether they work or not, so the system does not discourage employment directly. On the other hand, the general rise in retirement benefits in relation to mean earnings may be partly responsible for the fall in retirement ages since World War II, even though benefits are reduced for those who take early retirement.

The French system redistributes income both within and between generations. Within generations, the basic program for private industrial workers is partly subsidizing autonomous pension programs and those in the public sector. This is particularly troublesome in relation to public employees and to workers employed by nationalized industries, who are paid much higher pensions than those who are paid by the basic program.

Civil servants and managers of social security programs currently deny the existence of long-term problems. For that reason, there is almost no discussion of accumulating a funded reserve as part of a solution to future funding problems. Yet accumulating some reserve before deteriorating demographics make it impossible is probably the most important current reform which could cushion the future stresses to which the system will be subjected.

BACKGROUND

The first pension funds appeared in France in 1910 with the law creating worker and peasant retirement. Many enterprises organized private employee insurance programs for sickness, disability, and old age. These became mandatory with the 1930 social security law, which established a funded system with premiums paid equally by employer and employee and placed in individual accounts. Old-age social insurance was calculated on the basis of contributions over a worker's entire career; after thirty years he would receive a pension equal to 40 percent of his mean base salary. The program included a redistributive element, since a fraction of the contributions was allocated to a reserve fund in order to insure minimum pensions.

The system was inadequate for two reasons. To begin with, workers who reached age 65 in 1930 were not covered; second, the law required that pension fund reserves be invested in public bonds. Monetary depreciation, which started to be significant toward the end of the 1930s and became very strong in the 1940s, ravaged the system and greatly reduced its real accumulated assets. Although this experience gave currency in France to the idea that fully funded pensions cannot work in inflationary periods, the real problem was not inflation in itself, but the obligation to invest in fixed-income public securities which are particularly vulnerable to inflation.

This erroneous idea, along with the desire to provide pensions immediately—even without sufficient accumulated assets—led the legislature in 1945 to create a nationwide pay-as-you-go retirement system consisting of several different programs, a system which is still in effect today, although it has since been extended and supplemented.

OUTLINE OF THE SYSTEM

The general retirement insurance fund, the CNAV, is managed, with government guidance, by employer and employee representatives. Of the special retirement schemes not included in the CNAV—schemes with considerable variation in their benefits and contributions—the most important are the statutory programs covering civil servants and employees in the nationalized sector, and the independent programs for others excluded from the CNAV (see table 1).

Table 1

Mandatory Retirement System, 1977

Coverage	Contributors (millions)	Administrative organization	Number of contributors to each retiree	Mean annual pension (francs)[a]
Industrial and commercial employees	13.0	Basic old-age insurance (CNAV)	3.2	20,650
		Complementary programs (ARRCO[b], AGIRC[c])	3.9	
Self-employed: farmers, storekeepers, craftsmen	3.2	Private program	0.9	6,523
Civil servants and employees of nationalized enterprises	3.0	Statutory programs	1.4	29,000

Source: "Quel avenir pour les retraites des salariés du secteur privé?" *Entreprise et Progrès* (June 1979).

[a]Exchange rate, 5 January 1981: F = $0.226.

[b]ARRCO: Association des régimes de retraites complémentaires.

[c]AGIRC: Association générale des institutions de retraite des cadres.

The basic old-age insurance programs were progressively supplemented in the 1960s by complementary retirement programs negotiated without government intervention between employers' organizations and unions. Since they were jointly managed by representatives of employers and employees, they can be considered private organizations. These diverse pension funds were regrouped in 1972 into such national organizations as the Association des régimes de retraites complémentaires (ARRCO) for nonmanagerial workers and the Association générale des institutions de retraite des cadres (AGIRC) for managers, and in that year contributions were legally mandated for all workers. As a result, these organizations acquired a monopoly status without being nationalized.

Finally, the state-guaranteed minimum annual income of 17,000 francs (about $2,975 U.S.) for people aged 65 or more, regardless of their participation in a pension program, is financed partly out of general revenues and partly out of the basic program. In 1980, 2.7 million people, or approximately 18 percent of all pensioners, received a supplement to bring their incomes up to this minimum guaranteed level. The pensions of industrial and commercial employees are financed exclusively from contributions; those of civil servants, public sector workers, and independent professionals are heavily subsidized by the state, partly through transfers of contributions from industrial and commercial employees' programs. The government can and does transfer continuously from the basic program (CNAV) to help finance the deficits of the other statutory and autonomous programs.

In the basic program, a payroll tax of 8.20 percent is paid by the employer and 4.70 percent by the employee on net salaries ranging from a regulated minimum (salaire minimum interprofessionnel de croissance [SMIC]—in 1980, about F 14 per hour) up to a ceiling, the amount of which is revised each year. The ceiling was F 60,120 in 1980, compared to a mean annual net salary of F 53,000 (about $9,275 U.S.). For nonmanagers, contributions to the complementary programs consist of payroll taxes of 2.64 percent for employers and 1.76 percent for employees on salaries ranging between the minimum regulated wage and three times the basic program ceiling. For managers, the same rates apply to salaries in the bracket between the minimum wage and the basic program ceiling, but higher rates— 6.18 percent for employers and 2.06 percent for employees— apply to salaries between the ceiling and four times the ceiling (see table 2). Rates have increased significantly to finance the growth in benefits and the increased charges resulting from the aging of the population and the slowing of economic growth in the 1970s. Contributions today represent 9.00 percent of national income and 12.00 percent of earned income (see table 3).

Table 2

Contribution Rates for the General and Complementary Programs

Program	Rates (in %)		Annual tax base
	Employer	Employee	
General	8.20	4.70	SMIC[a] to ceiling[b]
Complementary:			
Nonmanagers			
(minimum)[c]	2.64	1.76	SMIC to ceiling-x-3
Managers	2.64	1.76	SMIC to ceiling
(minimum)	6.18	2.06	Ceiling to ceiling-x-4

[a]SMIC: *Salaire minimum interprofessionnel de croissance* (minimum wage).
[b]Ceiling: annual social security ceiling (60,120 francs in 1980).
[c]Minimum: mandatory minimum rate.

Table 3

Contributions, National Income, and Eearnings: Basic and Complementary Programs (combined)

Year	Contributions	
	As % of national income	As % of earnings[a]
1950	2.9	4.4
1955	3.1	4.6
1960	3.5	5.2
1965	4.7	7.0
1970	5.7	8.1
1975	7.5	9.6
1980	9.0	12.0

[a]Gross wage earnings plus income of self-employed people.

Since 1965 the number of beneficiaries has been growing more rapidly than the number of contributors, but the spectacular development of complementary retirement programs has enabled pensions to grow and has improved the pensioners' standard of living relative to that of contributors, as shown in table 4. During the 1970s, however, the ratio of contributors to pensioners declined for the complementary programs, while the slowing of the economy and the rise in unemployment—which amounted to 6 percent of the labor force in 1980—reduced income from contributions. All of these factors have combined to put a squeeze on the pension system.

Table 4

Ratio of Contributors to Beneficiaries:
Basic and Complementary Programs (combined)

Year	Basic programs	Complementary programs	Replacement rates[a]
1955	3.41	—	27.5
1960	3.39	—	27.4
1965	2.91	4.54	34.4
1970	2.29	2.92	37.4
1975	2.12	2.91	38.2
1980	1.80	2.51	41.9

[a]Mean pension as % of mean annual earnings.

Independent of business-cycle fluctuations and unemployment, more permanent problems have also appeared. The exceptionally favorable conditions which characterized the introduction of the redistributional pension system, including a decreasing median age in the years 1945-1965, have disappeared. Almost the entire labor force today has contributed both to the basic system and to a complementary program. The full range of contributors has been tapped, and the "chain letter" system is knocking against its demographic limits. Following a brief decline in the median age between 1980 and 1985, demographers foresee an aging of the population which will significantly accelerate after 2005. This development implies an increasing burden on employed workers to maintain currently legislated benefits (see table 5).

Table 5
Overall Ratio of Workers to Retirees
1950-2060[a]

	Year	Ratio at assumed birthrate[b]	
		(1.8)	(2.1)
Actual:	1950	4.62	4.62
	1955	4.17	4.17
	1960	3.69	3.69
	1965	3.38	3.38
	1970	3.14	3.14
	1975	2.66	2.66
Projected:	1985	2.82	2.82
	1990	2.70	2.70
	1995	2.60	2.60
	2000	2.49	2.50
	2005	2.39	2.43
	2010	2.24	2.33
	2015	2.04	2.16
	2020	1.86	2.01
	2025	1.72	1.93
	2030	1.64	1.87
	2035	1.58	1.85
	2040	1.56	1.86
	2045	1.58	1.90
	2050	1.59	1.91
	2055	1.61	1.93
	2060	1.63	1.95

[a]From 1950 to 1975 labor force participation rates are actual rates; after 1980 it is assumed that the rates observed in 1978 prevail.

[b]Current (1980) rate: 1.95.

Pensions in the basic program depend on the salary received during the ten best years of the insured's career, the number of years during which he paid contributions, and his retirement age—which may be anytime after 60 years. The official retirement age is 65, but it can be freely negotiated between employers and employees. The ten years' salary on which the pension level is based is expressed in francs of the retirement years. Twice a year, however, in January and July, the government revalues this basic pension in relation to an index of wage reimbursement for health insurance programs. Accordingly, pensions are not directly indexed against the price level. For the complementary programs, contributions paid during working years entitle beneficiaries to retirement "points" defined each year by the pension funds in order to equalize pensions and contributions.

Indexation thus is not built into the French social security system. It has nevertheless evolved by legislative discretion to accommodate inflation.

RECENT PERFORMANCE

The years 1950-1980 were particularly favorable to pensioners. The introduction of a pure pay-as-you-go pension system generally involves some redistribution to the first generation of pensioners, those who contributed less than their share. In addition, the sustained growth of the French economy in this period, as well as the initially favorable ratio of beneficiaries to contributors, permitted a 5.5 percent real annual growth in the average pension during this period.

LONG-TERM PERSPECTIVES

Based on these figures, the National Institute for Statistics (Institut national de la statistique et des études économiques [INSEE], see France 1980*b*) recently projected the functioning of the retirement system between the years 2000 and 2020, based on three sets of assumptions about labor force participation. The first set (1) assumes 1978 participation rates for women and people over age 60; the second (2) extrapolates into the future the recent strong growth in those participation rates; and the third (3) assumes that all people retire at 60 years of age.

Table 6 shows how the contributions would have to evolve as a percentage of gross domestic product (GDP) to maintain the 1977 replacement rate of 42.0 percent. The median projections for each assumed birthrate imply an increase in contributions

Table 6

**Projected Growth in the Mean Contribution Rate
as Percentage of GDP, Given a 42% Replacement Rate**

Assumed birthrate (1980: 1.95)	Labor force participation (assumption)	Year	
		2000	2020
	1	9.4	10.7
2.1	2	10.3	11.9
	3	11.1	13.0
	1	9.4	11.4
1.8	2	10.3	12.7
	3	11.2	13.4

as a percentage of GDP from 9.7 percent (actual) in 1977 to 11.9 percent in 2020 for the high birthrate and to 12.7 percent for the lower one. If the 1977 contribution/GDP ratio of 9.7 percent is maintained, the replacement rate must decline substantially (see table 7). These figures suggest the need for a choice between taxes and standards of living. A heavier tax burden on earnings will be required to maintain pensioners' relative living standards; maintaining current tax rates will require reducing their relative living standards.

Table 7

Projected Evolution of the Replacement Rate[a]
Given a 9.7% Contribution Rate

Assumed birthrate (1980: 1.95)	Labor force participation (assumption)	Year	
		2000	2020
2.1	1	44	37
	2	39	33
	3	36	30
1.8	1	44	35
	2	39	31
	3	36	29

[a]Average benefits as a proportion of average earnings.

The apparent rate of return calculated by comparing contributions and benefits over an entire lifetime will fall progressively in future years (see table 8). The return drops significantly for the youngest generations because of the disappearance of the "free gift" obtained by those who first entered the pay-as-you-go pension system. This simulation shows that, for the generation now entering the labor force, the rate of return to pay-as-you-go old-age insurance will lie close to the rate of growth in per capital income. No major catastrophe thus appears to wait on the horizon within the range of reasonable assumptions: a progressively aging population and steady growth of per capita income in a reasonable range by historical standards—0 percent being extremely pessimistic and 4 percent, overly optimistic. Nonetheless, the forthcoming decline in rates of return may have even stronger implications in the more distant future.

After the year 2020, the projected demographic situation will continue to deteriorate, though less so. It is important to note, however, that these numbers assume relatively constant life expectancies—sustaining relatively constant retirement periods.

Table 8

Projected Annual Percentage Rate of Return to Old-Age Insurance at Ages 20-45 in 1980[a]

Assumed birthrate (1980: 1.95)	Age	Productivity growth rates		
		0%	2%	4%
2.1	45	2.23	3.87	5.51
	40	1.52	3.32	5.12
	35	0.90	2.77	4.65
	30	0.35	2.30	4.26
	25	0.12	2.15	4.10
	20	0.04	2.05	4.06
1.8	45	2.15	3.79	5.43
	40	1.37	3.16	4.96
	35	0.66	2.62	4.41
	30	0.10	1.99	3.95
	25	—0.20	1.76	3.79
	20	—0.40	1.60	3.63

Source: Picot 1980.

[a]Contribution rate: 11.8% from 1980 to 2050. This rate is the ratio of total contributions to gross earnings (wages and salaries plus gross income of self-employed people) and is higher than the ratio of contributions to GDP or national income.

If life expectancies should increase even a couple of years, the future consequences would be even more serious. In the end, the effects of population aging will be felt mainly by people now under age 20 who will enter the labor force in the 1980s and 1990s; their rate of return will be even lower than those computed in table 8 for older people.

The long-term projection is that the rate of return will keep falling, as will retirees' standard of living relative to that of the working population. A sharp increase in the contribution rate, the "solution" practiced during the past thirty years, will be impractical in the long term since—with the accumulated debt growing faster than contributions that workers would reasonably be willing to pay—it would lead to bankruptcy.

IMPACTS ON THE OVERALL ECONOMY

It is not completely clear now that the system of mandatory pensions has changed levels of saving or affected the labor supply, so we cannot assess its significant consequences for the growth of the economy.

Effects on saving

The mechanism of pay-as-you-go does not result in the accumulation of investable resources. Contributions are immediately redistributed to retirees, who spend them principally for consumption. In some countries, such as Sweden, pay-as-you-go pension funds also accumulate contingency reserve funds and have partial recourse to a fully funded mechanism. Some French pension funds have taken analogous although extremely weak precautions, but in general the French system functions overwhelmingly on the pay-as-you-go principle.

For the contributor or pensioner, however, contributions and pensions, by transferring purchasing power from working to retirement years, assure the same result as personal savings. Thus each increase in mandatory contributions reduces national savings to the extent that current workers trust future generations to maintain the system and to repay them, when they retire, for the sacrifices they are now making for today's pensioners.

The introduction and development of a pay-as-you-go system therefore reduces national saving and investment in favor of current consumption. Investment declines, which in turn slows growth and imposes higher contribution rates on future generations to provide pensions equal to today's.

There are also countervailing effects, however. Mandatory retirement with coverage tends to stimulate active workers to retire earlier, thus encouraging them to save more during their working lives in order to provide for a longer period of retirement. And some authors have argued that current contributors, anticipating higher pensions when they retire, know that

these will be paid by their children; consequently, they save
more now in order to bequeath more wealth to alleviate the
burden on the next generation. The net result of all these
effects on present savings is uncertain.

Another argument along the same lines is that the mandatory pay-as-you-go system simply replaces redistribution within families and through public or private charitable organizations. Since these forms of redistribution did not accumulate
savings either, substituting one transfer system for another has
not necessarily affected the overall saving rate.

Attempts to verify empirically the effects of pay-as-you-go
pension systems on saving are the subject of a lively controversy in the United States (particularly between Feldstein
[1974] and Barro [1974]). In France, only two such studies exist
to date, and they arrive at almost opposite conclusions.
According to Kessler and Strauss-Kahn (see France 1980a), the
development of retirement programs has had no significant
effect on saving. On the other hand, Picot (1980) finds an
appreciable reduction in saving: for the year 1978, the total
retirement contributions of F 170 billion reduced savings by between F 70 and 110 billion. Given that total savings for that
year were F 275 billion, the retirement programs induced a
drop of between 25 percent and 40 percent.

It is not yet possible to draw any solid conclucions because
of methodological problems with these studies. It is clear that
more work is needed, because this is a crucial issue.

Effects on employment

Receipt of a pension in France does not preclude holding
full-time paid employment, in contrast to other countries.
Nevertheless, like other countries, France has experienced a
fall in retirement ages since World War II, even though benefits are lower for younger pensioners. There are no accurate
studies of the effects of the pension system on the participation
in the labor force of people over age 60. We are thus limited to
noting—without ascribing causality—the correlation between

the progressive rise in pensions relative to mean earnings and the drop in average age of retirement.

REDISTRIBUTIVE EFFECTS

Mandatory pay-as-you-go pension systems have several redistributional effects. The most frequently discussed in France is the particularly visible one of state transfers between the various programs. In 1977, F 3.4 billion were deducted from the national old-age insurance fund, which covers only workers in industry and commerce, to finance nearly half of the minimum old-age pension. Similarly, F 2.6 billion from the same fund were used to subsidize the public sector and autonomous pension programs. In toto, F 6.0 billion, or more than 10 percent, were transferred from the nearly F 52.0 billion in receipts of the general program. The mean pension paid by independent programs is less than the mean of those paid in the general program because the number of active farm workers and craftsmen is declining rapidly, thus increasing the pensioner/contributor ratio. But the statutory programs for public employees and for workers employed by nationalized industries pay much higher average pensions than those of the general program. Since these groups refuse to pay for their own high pensions, industrial and commercial workers are subsidizing the pensions of the already well-off civil service and nationalized sectors.

Another important redistributional impact occurs when the government changes the wage ceiling on which contributions are based. Contributions to the complementary pension scheme for managers in industry and commerce are based on higher payroll taxes levied on income between the ceiling and four times the ceiling. Therefore, when the ceiling rises faster than inflation, more receipts flow to the basic program, thereby reducing the income base of the managers' complementary programs because of the reduced dispersion of wages on which supplementary payroll taxes are levied and the small number of very high wages. In the extreme case, a very high ceiling would empty the tax bracket from which the complementary programs draw most of their revenues, diverting income to the general program.

While the continuing debate concentrates on the redistribution of contributions, studies of the system's long-term prospects frequently leave problems of intergenerational redistribution unexamined. This curious bias can be explained by the structural incentives faced by the pension industry. Pension organizations, unlike business corporations, have no equity reflecting the actualized value of future streams of expenses and receipts and cannot easily assess the soundness of their financial position and performance. Moreover, the government has granted these private nonprofit organizations—which are run by representatives of employers, employees, and civil servants—the equivalent of a legal right to levy taxes. Each social security program has the right to tax a portion of the working population. Protecting and extending this right are thus of more immediate interest to managers than are long-term prospects.

This probably explains why, unlike their colleagues in other countries which make use of voluntary insurance and partially funded mechanisms, French specialists on these matters tend at the outset to exclude any consideration of funding, even as a complement to the current system. The evidence notwithstanding, they argue that we should expect no serious difficulties in financing future pensions on a pay-as-you-go basis.

This distrust of fully funded pensions has longstanding origins, as we have seen. It is ill founded, however. Authorization should be given for a wider range of pension investments. There is no reason, for instance, in a demographically static or aging society, why the investment performance of funded pension programs should not be as good as that of a pay-as-you-go system. Portfolios including diversified assets—particularly real estate, land, and geographically dispersed bonds and shares—stand up quite well under inflationary conditions.

Full funding also offers certain advantages over pay-as-you-go. Under the latter, a pensioner's income depends on demographics and on the level of economic activity during his retirement. With the former it depends on the rates of return of various financial instruments over his entire working life and part of his retirement. Economic risks are thus better distributed and demographic uncertainties have no direct importance (except indirectly, by modifying the rates of return on investment assets).

We cannot, of course, envisage converting the system in its entirety; this would be too costly. But the disappointing prospects for pay-as-you-go will tempt young people who enter the system from now on to look for more individual choice in saving—that is, to rely on more private saving mechanisms. Partial funding is needed today to avoid overloading the generations which will be working after the year 2010. It would seem appropriate to divide the financial cost of pensions—which will rise dramatically during this period—among different generations. This could be at least partly accomplished by accumulating a capital fund, collective or individual, between 1980 and 2000, when the contributor/beneficiary ratio—although already rather low—will not be too unfavorable. Several different ways could be used: increasing the retirement age, reducing the growth of current pensions, or—following the examples of Switzerland and Germany—mandating formation of complementary private saving schemes which would constitute a third private component of the retirement system. Alternatively, in the years after 2010 pensioners and workers could accept reduced pensions or increased contributions. In any case, the spreading of these costs will be done better the sooner it starts. For this reason, the long-term problem of retirement pensions is in fact an immediate problem.

CONCLUSION

Until recently, the system established in France in 1945 has provided extremely effective retirement protection for the elderly. The exceptionally favorable factors associated with the various programs at their inception are now rapidly disappearing. After gaining remarkable benefits for successive generations and governments, the system now threatens us with a future of rising costs. The question of distributing these costs raises serious political difficulties which will be aggravated if we simply shove them off onto future generations. Some modest measures taken today would permit progressive reduction in the debts uncautiously accumulated over the past thirty years. The time to act is now.

3

RICHARD HEMMING
JOHN A. KAY

Great Britain

National Insurance and the Beveridge Report. Occupational
pensions, inflation, indexation. State Earnings Related Pension Scheme (SERPS). Contracting out and the contribution
rate. Pay-as-you-go, reserve funding, saving, and investment.
Increasing costs and the earnings rule. Income redistribution.
The impact of social security.

The British pension system is one of the most complex in the world, principally because it combines an extensive network of private occupational pension programs with a comparable state scheme. The state program (State Earnings Related Pension Scheme—SERPS), introduced in 1978, has two elements —a basic, mandatory component which pays a flat pension amount independent of prior income, and a supplementary component related to past earnings. Employees who are covered by approved private occupational programs may contract out of the supplementary state program, and roughly 90.0 percent of those eligible have done so. The state makes up the difference when private scheme benefits fall short of those under the state scheme. Altogether, total benefits in the mandatory social security program amount to about 10.7 percent of gross national product (GNP), of which 5.5 percent goes to retirement pensions. Private retirement insurance equals another 5.0 percent.

The state program is a pay-as-you-go system financed partly by a payroll tax and partly by a direct subsidy from general revenues amounting to about 15.00 percent of total program expenditures. The current overall tax rate is 20.45 percent (6.75 percent paid by the employee and 13.70 percent paid by the employer, but including a special surtax) of earnings up to £165 per week ($318 U.S. [£ = $1.93 as of 1 July 1981]). Seven percent is taken off for those who contract out of the supplementary program.

When the program has matured, single pensioners who are full members (at age 60 for women, 65 for men) will receive a flat-rate basic pension which averages 23 percent of average earnings (20 percent for men, 32 percent for women), plus a supplement equal to 25 percent of the best twenty years' average of revalued earnings between £23 ($44 U.S.) and £165 per week. (An index of average earnings is used for revaluation purposes.) A man whose wife is not entitled to a pension in her own right will receive an additional flat-rate pension equal to approximately 70 percent of the single rate. Both pensions and earnings limits are indexed to inflation.

While current demographic trends are relatively favorable to the new program, the future ratio of workers to retirees will decline, even if fertility rates rise to levels which at this point seem unlikely (2.1 births per family). On the other hand, if fertility rates continue at recently experienced levels (1.8 per family), the worker-to-retiree ratio will fall from 2.8 to 2.0 fifty years from now. Even modest improvements in mortality rates could reduce the ratio well below 2.0. In this event, payroll tax rates could rise to more than 30 percent to finance currently legislated benefits. While the political and economic implications are uncertain, it is clear that such results would be extremely serious for the system as a whole.

No current evidence exists that state pensions have depressed private saving and investment in the United Kingdom, but the available data refer to a period when state pensions were not related to earnings, so no effect on savings should have been expected from the old system. The new scheme, however, may well have a more significant impact.

SERPS has an earnings test for five years after the official retirement age. With earnings up to about 50 percent of the average (or up to £52 per week), pensions are exempt from tax. A 50 percent tax applies to pensions for a small band of earnings above that amount (i.e., between £52 and £56 per week), and higher earnings raise the marginal taxe rate on pensions to

100 percent. The earnings test thus provides a clear disincentive to full-time work for people immediately after they reach the official retirement age, but many people work part time, for which the penalty is less severe. It is likely that SERPS will reduce employment even more when the scheme matures and pays more generous pensions than it does at present.

The redistributional impact across generations under the new system is broadly similar to that of the other countries discussed in this volume. Within generations, the largest redistribution is to women pensioners, who can retire five years earlier and who, on average, live longer than men.

The present arrangements command general support, but if they fail to meet evident problems or to respond to new requirements, the future development of the system may again become a political issue. If so, further responsible reform will be extremely difficult, because its implementation would require more than the lifetime of a single government.

A BRIEF HISTORY

Social security pensions have been paid in Britain since 1908. They were originally simple transfer payments made to low-income people from general revenues, but by World War II the system had been gradually extended and liberalized. Piecemeal reforms, however, had resulted in a social security system with no coherent rationale. It had become a combination of insurance and transfer system whereby some of the retired, unemployed, and sick received benefits as of right because they had made contributions, while others—having paid little or nothing—had to demonstrate need.

After the war the system was reformed along lines suggested in the Beveridge Report (Great Britain 1942). For most of the postwar period the British system has provided retirement, unemployment, sickness and disability benefits as of right to those who have made adequate contributions to the National Insurance scheme. This group includes all those with a reasonably continuous record of employment as well as the self-employed. Along with family allowances, free health care, and a government commitment to full employment, the scheme was originally expected to eradicate poverty by the mid-1960s. In the interim a means-tested benefit, National Assistance, was made available to those not adequately covered by National Insurance.

The National Insurance scheme was established as a pay-as-you-go system financed by flat-rate contributions and providing flat-rate benefits. In the beginning neither contributions nor benefits were related to earnings. While Beveridge's intention was for benefit entitlements to accumulate gradually, thereby building up a partial fund, in practice full entitlements were conferred immediately, though at lower levels. The ratio of the retired to the working population increased considerably after 1948, which led to a rapid increase in costs. Since the Exchequer was unwilling to subsidize the scheme out of general revenue beyond an initially agreed level, the flat-rate contribution had to be rapidly increased. This placed an inacceptable burden on those with low incomes, and in 1961 a small earnings-related scheme was introduced as a revenue-raising device.

The 1960s saw growing public and official concern about social welfare, and in particular about the performance of income maintenance policies. Beveridge had intended that National Insurance benefits such as retirement pensions would take people above the poverty line, but this objective was defeated by the initial decision to pay lower benefits to all. Pensioners without significant other income were therefore entitled to a means-tested supplementary pension (National Assistance), but many did not take it because it retained the stigma of prewar means-tested benefits. As a result, many of the retired were poor and many of the poor were retired.

A solution to this problem, along with a remedy for the scheme's poor financial state, was sought in a new earnings-related scheme, designed from first principles and finally enacted in 1978 as the State Earnings Related Pension Scheme (SERPS; see Great Britain 1974).

OCCUPATIONAL PENSIONS

Adequate description and informative discussion of the new state scheme is difficult without some background knowledge of occupational pension arrangements in Britain. As is clear from table 1, the coverage of such arrangements has increased rapidly since the war. Approximately half of all employees are now members of an occupational pension scheme, and coverage is somewhat better in the public sector than in the private. This rapid development has been stimulated by the considerable tax advantages drawn from schemes which receive Inland Revenue approval, for which the principal condition is that benefits should not exceed rather generous maxima. Contributions are paid out of pretax income, and if the scheme is funded—as is the case in the private sector and part of the public sector—the income and capital gains of the fund are not

Table 1

Employees in Occupational Schemes, 1954-1979
(in millions)

Year	Private sector		Public sector		Labor force	
	Men	Women	Men	Women	Total	Total
1954	2.5	0.6	2.4	0.7	6.2	24.2
1956	3.5	0.8	2.9	0.8	8.0	24.7
1963	6.4	0.8	3.0	0.9	11.1	25.7
1967	6.8	1.3	3.1	1.0	12.2	25.9
1971	5.5	1.3	3.2	1.1	11.1	25.1
1975	4.9	1.1	3.7	1.7	11.4	25.8
1979	4.7	1.5	3.8	1.8	11.8	26.4

Source: Great Britain 1981.

liable to tax. Tax-advantaged schemes typically offer pensions of one-half to two-thirds final salary.

Concern has been expressed about two aspects of private pension arrangements in Britain. First, Britain has become accustomed to high inflation and there seems little prospect of price stability being reestablished in the foreseeable future. Public sector occupational schemes which operate on a pay-as-you-go basis—only certain local government employees and employees of the public corporations are in funded schemes—have generous indexation provisions. Some of these schemes are supposed to be subject to the disciplines of funding, but this is seldom the case in practice. On realistic assumptions about future investment returns and inflation, the contributions paid are hardly sufficient to finance the pensions promised. While most funded schemes have increased pensions to take account of inflation, a formal commitment to even partial indexation is rare. Most schemes already carry a limited liability for indexation, since pensions are related to final salary; to enhance this by guaranteeing indexed pensions, when future inflation rates are unknown and indexed investments are not available to hedge them, is hardly practical. Thus the indexation of pensions received by members of funded occupational schemes is usually discretionary, and this puts them at a disadvantage relative to the indexation provisions granted members of some public sector occupational schemes.

Second, there is a perception that occupational pension schemes are unfair to individuals who leave their jobs. The most blatant shortcomings—which were clearly in the interests of the schemes' architects but were adverse to the wider public interest—have been corrected. But the provisions permitting people to change jobs without losing pension rights remain inadequate. While preservation of pension rights is required for employees whose service exceeds five years, such preservation is based only on nominal salary at the time of leaving. Those who stay with the same employer can expect to have such rights related to final salary, which will be higher because of sub-

sequent real earnings growth and also because of inflation in
the interim. The present situation is not only inequitable, but is
a serious impediment to labor mobility.

THE NEW STATE SCHEME

Although there had long been widespread agreement that a
state and private "partnership" was necessary, the difficulty of
meeting disparate political demands prevented effective social
security reforms for twenty years, until 1978. Pressure for a
new scheme with earnings-related contributions came from
mounting concern about the growing burden of still predominantly flat-rate contributions on low-income people. Pressure for earnings-related benefits came in part from a desire to
give the population as a whole the advantages already enjoyed
by professional groups and public sector employees through
occupational pension schemes.

The State Earnings Related Pension Scheme is a pay-as-you-
go system financed partly by National Insurance contributions
levied on both employees and employers and partly by a transfer from general revenue amounting to about 15.00 percent of
total program costs. The contribution rate on full members is
6.75 percent on earnings up to £165 per week, and the contribution rate on employers is 13.70 percent on the same earnings,
including a 3.50 percent surcharge. The surcharge does not
finance National Insurance benefits, but almost exactly offsets
the Exchequer's contribution from general revenue; it is therefore appropriate to view the total contribution rate as
20.45 percent. Once the scheme has matured, a single pensioner who is a full member of SERPS will receive a basic flat-rate
pension—currently equal to £23 per week—which is approximately 23.00 percent of average earnings (20.00 percent for
men, 32.00 percent for women), plus an additional component
equal to 25.00 percent of the average of the best twenty years'
revalued earnings in the range £23-£165 per week. An index of
average earnings is used for revaluation purposes. Men and

women have equal pension status, except that pensions are paid to women aged 60 and over and to men aged 65 and over. A male pensioner whose wife is not entitled to a pension in her own right receives an additional flat-rate pension of approximately 70.00 percent of the single rate. Pensions are indexed to retail prices, and so are the earnings limits.

Full membership in SERPS is not compulsory. Employees who are otherwise insured under approved occupational schemes may contract out of the earnings-related component of SERPS while retaining the basic component and certain other benefits. The decision to contract out is taken by the employer and binds all members of that particular scheme. For those who contract out, the joint contribution rate is reduced by 7 percent. This is sufficient to induce the contracting out of 10.3 million employes, roughly 90 percent of eligible employees.

Approval to contract out is granted only to schemes which are capable of providing a pension equivalent to the earnings-related SERPS entitlement but based upon average lifetime revalued earnings rather than the average of the best twenty years' revalued earnings. The state then makes up the difference between these two figures, and makes additional payments to provide indexation of the earnings-related pension that would have been paid under SERPS. Contracted-out employees still receive substantial earnings-related benefits under the new scheme.

THE COST OF SERPS

Although very few earnings-related pensions are paid at the moment, National Insurance contributions amount to around 20 percent of payroll, offsetting the surcharge against the Exchequer's contribution from general revenue. The lower and upper wage limits (which define the range of income on which the payroll taxes are levied) reduce the tax base only very little. Although higher social security taxes are found in many European countries, the size of this tax as a cost of employment is causing increasing concern. Further increases could have adverse effects. It is therefore important to calculate how much contributions are expected to rise to finance the mature scheme and what levels they can be expected to reach in the next century.

Public expenditure on the provision of social security benefits has been demanding an increasing share of gross national product (see table 2). Roughly half of this total is accounted for by the provision of retirement pensions. When SERPS was first proposed, the combined contribution rate for the existing National Insurance scheme was expected to reach approximately 14.00 percent of earnings up to an earnings limit, ignoring the surcharge, by 1978.[1] Given that a 7.00 percent contracting-out rebate was to be paid under the new scheme, it was estimated that the contribution rate would have to rise immediately to 16.50 percent (the current rate, excluding the surcharge, is 16.95 percent); it would be 17.50 percent in 1998, when full earnings-related pensions first became payable, and would reach 18.50 percent in 2008. Beyond 2008 the projections become somewhat vague. It was conjectured that the contribution rate may have to rise 2.00 percent by 2018 to become 20.50 percent, with the possibility of even further increases thereafter.

Table 2

**Aggregate Expenditure on Social Security Benefits
(in percent)**

Year	All social security benefits as % of gross national product	Retirement pensions as % of all social security benefits
1951	5.5	38.2
1961	6.7	47.2
1971	8.7	45.2
1977	10.7	48.5

Source: Great Britain 1979.

In our opinion, these estimates are too low, even allowing for some cost savings that will be made as the scheme matures;[2]

furthermore, by examining only the period up to 2008 in any detail, an important source of potential cost escalation receives only scant attention. Consider this second point first.

It is clear from Table 3 that in its first thirty years demographic factors are relatively favorable to the scheme. In common with a large number of other countries, the dependency ratio—the ratio of the working population to pensioners—has declined substantially in the last thirty years, but no such fall is expected

Table 3

Ratio of Working Population to Pensioners

Year	Low fertility (= 1.8)	Actual	High fertility (= 2.1)
1951	—	3.37	—
1961	—	3.13	—
1971	—	2.84	—
1981	2.76	—	2.76
1991	2.87	—	2.87
2001	2.99	—	3.03
2011	2.84	—	2.99
2023	2.41	—	2.66
2028	2.19	—	2.49
2032	2.04	—	2.40

Source: Ermisch 1980.

in the next thirty. Thereafter there will be some decrease as the relatively numerous generation born in the period 1945-1965 reaches retirement age. These calculations, however, assume stable mortality rates among pensioners. The high fertility projection now shows a rather modest decline in the dependency ratio, but the low fertility projection shows a far more serious trend. The trends will be still worse with even modest improvement in life expectancies. Indeed, from around 2.8 at the outset of SERPS, with only a modest mortality improvement the dependency ratio could fall to well below 2.0. This could have far-reaching implications.

There are two principal reasons for believing that the cost estimates that have been provided for 1998 and 2008 are too low. The first concerns the benefit formula. Pensions are based on revalued earnings in the best twenty years of working life, while the contributions which pay for them are based on the average earnings of the working population at the date they are paid. Hence the required contribution rate is sensitive to the amount by which the average of the best twenty years' earnings exceeds average lifetime earnings. The official projections use what is no more than a rule of thumb to estimate the size of this difference and the rate at which full benefit entitlements are built up. In our view, the chosen rule of thumb is inappropriate and underestimates the costs of the best twenty years' provision. This affects not only the benefits paid to full members of SERPS but also those received by contracted-out employees.[3]

The second reason concerns the impact of contracting out. A high incidence of contracting out raises the contribution rate in the short run, since the 7 percent rebate has to be financed with no corresponding reduction in concurrent benefits. The official view is that contracting out in the long run holds down contribution rates and may even reduce them. Our view is that contracting out raises the contribution rate in both the short run and the long run. This is because, in the long run, the contribution rate required for a pay-as-you-go scheme is higher—or lower—than the contribution rate under a fully funded scheme to the extent that real investment returns are positive or negative. It is intended that contracting out should only be profitable at a small positive real return; we believe that the state benefits paid to contracted-out employees have been underestimated, and that contracting out makes sense even at a small negative return. This is because the state guarantees indexation of benefits for contracted-out employees. Official calculations are based on projections of the inflation rate prescribed by the government, which in the past have been systematically underestimated. Contracting out thus is more extensive than antic-

ipated, despite negative investment returns, and the joint
contribution rate is correspondingly higher. It now stands at
17 percent, excluding the surcharge.

We believe that demographic changes, the cost of the best
twenty years' provision, and the continuation of high rates of
inflation in the British economy could combine to make the
new state pension scheme much more expensive than many
people anticipate. Only careful research can reveal the range of
feasible contribution rates, and this must now be a priority if
the future of the scheme is to be the subject of sensible discussion.

PAY-AS-YOU-GO FUNDING

Should the new state scheme be revealed as potentially
costly, the extensively discussed issue of the relative merits of
pay-as-you-go and funding may attract further attention. Unfortunately, the arguments so far have been rather confused. A
major concern is to show that one method or the other is
"cheaper"; but from the national economic perspective, the
cost of pension provision is determined by the size of the promised benefits and not by the financial arrangements which are
made to secure them. The method of provision, however, may
have implications for the rates of saving and investment.

SAVING AND INVESTMENT

If a fully funded social security pension scheme—earning the
market rate of interest—were introduced, then in principle it
would be a perfect substitute for other forms of retirement
saving. Introducing a funded social security pension system
therefore would leave aggregate saving and investment unaffected. If individual perceptions were sufficiently sophis-
ticated, then the introduction of an unfunded scheme would
have the same impact; anticipating the social security pension,

people would save less in other forms. Current contributions would be lower, but future contributions would be higher. Individuals, perceiving that their current increases in net income were at the expense of their and their children's future net income, would increase their saving. In practice, however, it is hard to take this ultrarational model seriously. It thus seems reasonable to conclude that the substitution of public pay-as-you-go for private funding depresses the levels of saving and investment.

However, there is a potential offset. In the absence of a social security pension scheme, some individuals might have worked until they were physically incapable of continuing. Compulsory membership in a pension scheme, on the other hand, may induce many people to plan an earlier and longer retirement, thereby increasing their saving. In the standard life-cycle model of saving behavior in which individuals plan to leave the world having consumed their lifetime resources, the conflicting influences of savings replacement and induced retirement lead to the conclusion that the saving response to membership in an unfunded pension scheme is theoretically indeterminate.

There are some celebrated but hotly disputed results for the United States which suggest that social security pensions considerably depressed aggregate saving (see Feldstein 1974; Munnell 1974). Critics have argued, however, that the time series data on which this result is based include a period when coverage was expanding rapidly and contributors failed to take account of inevitable cost increases; that the impact of social security cannot be separated from other influences on saving; that allowing for intergenerational transfers completely mitigates the result; and that the result is explained wholly by computing error.[4] Little purpose woulf be served by attempting to resolve the debate here. On the other hand, it is true that postwar United Kingdom data reveal no evidence that social security pensions have depressed saving (see von Furstenberg 1979; Hemming 1978). These data, however, refer to a period when social security pensions represented flat-rate provision of an income below the official poverty line. The earnings-related scheme may well have a more significant impact on saving.

THE EARNINGS RULE AND PARTICIPATION

In the absence of social security pensions, people would plan to retire at different ages. While some people may not be directly induced to retire by the allure of a retirement pension, work can be made to appear relatively unattractive. For five years after the official retirement age (up to 65 for women and 70 for men) earned income is heavily taxed; there is no tax on pensions up to around 50 percent of average earnings (up to £52 per week), but a small band is then taxed at a marginal rate of 50 percent (between £52 and £56 per week), and above this the marginal tax rate on pensions is 100 percent. This is a clear disincentive to full participation in the labor force after the official retirement age. But the disincentive to work part time is less, and this is a popular option among younger pensioners, especially those without an occupational pension.

U.S. studies have shown that participation decisions are affected by social security pensions and the earnings rule. There are some marked disincentive effects. Another pre-SERPS study in the United Kingdom shows that both men's and women's participation decisions respond to social security pensions and the earnings rule, much as economic theory would predict (see Zabalza et al. 1980*a*). In general, the impact of the former is far greater than that of the latter, and women are more responsive to financial incentives than men. We can expect SERPS to reduce participation in the work force in the future because pensions will be significantly more generous once the scheme has matured. This greater generosity is particularly evident for women. And a pension costs rise, it is possible that the earnings rule will be made more severe, although recent changes have been in the opposite direction.

DISTRIBUTIONAL CONSIDERATIONS

Distributional impacts of a pension scheme are typically divided into three categories. First is the impact at a point in time. If contributions and pensions are not proportional to the current incomes of contributors and pensioners, respectively, the cross-sectional distribution of income is affected. SERPS contributions are, in fact, more or less proportional to income; pensioners on average are poorer than the working population, and richer pensioners are more likely to be contracted out of SERPS and to have lower social security pensions relative to their other income. In this sense, the scheme generally involves a progressive transfer between generations—from younger, richer generations to older, poorer ones—and is progressive within a generation of pensioners. The other two redistributive aspects, however—across individual lifetimes and between individuals with different lifetime incomes—are much more significant. We will consider them in turn.

Social security pensions may be viewed as a forced saving program. If—as is certainly the case in Britain—society in any event will intervene to prevent retirement incomes falling substantially below the poverty line, it is reasonable to compel individuals to purchase at least some of the insurance they could otherwise freely ignore. If they can afford it, they should be made to set aside something towards a basic retirement pension. Government intervention and compulsory participation make benefits available on more favorable terms than are offered by private insurance companies.

If private insurance were widely available on the terms set by the government, the rich would typically wish to purchase more than the poor. Earnings-related contributions and pensions acknowledge this. And if the scheme is to be progressive in lifetime incomes, the poor will be offered a higher rate of return on their contributions than the rich. Social security therefore will have the effect of redistributing, both over individual lifetimes and from people with high lifetime incomes to those with low lifetime incomes. This cannot be achieved in a systematic way by any other fiscal mechanism in Britain.

Despite its progressivity in the standard—but limited—sense, in its present form SERPS is most unlikely to be progressive in any reasonable concept of lifetime income. Broadly speaking, lifetime contributions are proportional to lifetime income; but because lifetime pension receipts are based upon the best twenty years' earnings, which need not be systematically related to lifetime income, the relationship between rates of return and lifetime income is arbitrary. Rates of return are more closely related to how much earnings vary over a life-time—or, more specifically, to the difference between the average of the best twenty years and the lifetime average. Differential mortality also means the rich benefit more from the system than the poor, since the rich live longer than the poor. By far the largest redistribution, however, is to women. They retire earlier, live longer, and on average contribute substantially less than men with identical pension entitlements.

CONCLUSIONS

The elaborate partnership of state and occupational sectors we have described appears to be relatively stable at present. But we should not be complacent. There are problems facing the partnership. Perhaps the most important is the inadequacy of transferability provisions. Improving the situation comes up against two difficulties. One is the cost; but if the price of remedying this unfairness and inefficiency in the distribution of pension rights is lower pensions for all, then so be it. The second is the difficulty employers face in funding indexed liabilities for former employees; this is indeed a serious problem, and its only apparent solution is a growth of opportunities to hedge indexed liabilities, either through the government or the private sector. The prospects of an extensive development of this king seem low. The only alternative is to expand the role of social security pensions relative to that of occupational schemes.

The retirement age is also a matter of concern. There is little attempt to defend the higher age of retirement for men than for women; it is a provision which arose almost accidentally in the course of World War II. But to raise the retirement age for women would violate firmly held expectations. A more politically feasible solution would be more flexible retirement ages for all, with actuarial adjustments to pensions or contributions reflecting the chosen date of retirement.

As it stands, the partnership of the state and private sectors probably implies significantly higher levels of future contributions than have been generally recognized. But in the absence of any marked decline in the dependency ratio—say, to 2.0 or thereabouts—these should not be unsustainable. The combined pressure of a lower dependency ratio, however, an extension of the role of SERPS to protect those who change jobs, and the introduction of flexible retirement ages could change this. It may then be time—if it was not before—to ask a more fundamental question about the British pension system.

In Britain, many obstacles have been put in the way of individual provision for retirement, particularly the high tax rates imposed on nominal—rather than real—investment income while the government has obstructed the development of indexation. In contrast, the tax system and legislation have strongly favored the compulsory collective provision for retirement. We believe that the pension system now makes greater provision for some people than they would make if they were free to choose for themselves. This may also be true in aggregate. We are not convinced that Britain has chosen the right course by encouraging substitution of compulsory social security provision for private saving rather than freeing the capital market to allow individuals to make such provision for themselves. At a time of growing concern about Britain's slow rate of economic growth, we are also concerned that its social security system is accentuating that pattern by fostering an inefficient allocation of lifetime resources and investment opportunities.

4

ONORATO CASTELLINO

Italy

Multiple programs in the system. Eligibility and deficits. "General" scheme; self-employed scheme. Overindexation of benefits. Saving and investment. Effect on employment; the underground economy. Distribution of benefits. The tax of inflation. The need for reform.

The Italian state pensions system consists of a large number of separate programs covering different sectors of the labor force. These include a "general" program for private sector employees, schemes for government employees, and three principal plans for the self-employed. Each of these programs has distinct payroll tax rates, conditions of entitlement, and benefit levels. Even within the general scheme, there are separate rules for farm employees and domestic servants. Pensions for all government programs now amount to about 12 percent of the gross national product (GNP), and there is almost no private retirement insurance.

The general program is by far the largest, with 12.0 million insured workers out of a total work force of 21.4 million. That program is financed on a pay-as-you-go basis by a payroll tax of 24.20 percent (17.05 percent on employers, 7.15 percent on employees), with no ceiling on the earnings to which the tax applies. But even this high payroll tax rate is not sufficient to finance program costs. The balance, amounting in 1980 to 13.00 percent of total general program costs, is absorbed as part of a growing national debt.

Pensions are payable to men at age 60 and to women at 55, subject to fifteen years' payment of contributions. An individual's pension is calculated at 2 percent of his last salary (averaged over his last three working years) for every year of contributions; 80 percent of last salary (the replacement rate) is the maximum pension allowable. There is also a guaranteed floor equal to 30 percent of industrial workers' current minimum wage.

The state employees' scheme is even more generous. Contributions to this and to public enterprise retirement programs covered only about 30.00 percent of total program costs in 1980, and these chronic program deficits are paid out of the general treasury. In the state employees' scheme, men become eligible for a pension after twenty years, regardless of their age, and married women after fifteen years. An individual's pension amounts to roughly 2.35 percent of his last salary for every year of contributions, up to a maximum of 94.00 percent. The guaranteed floor is about 60.00 percent of public employees' current minimum wage.

Programs for the self-employed also exist, covering more than 5 million workers. These also are financed on a pay-as-you-go basis, combining a payroll tax with substantial transfers from general revenues (amounting to more than 60 percent of program benefits in 1980). Altogether, aggregated contributions to all retirement programs cover only about 70 percent of combined program benefits, with the other 30 percent made up by direct transfers from public budgets.*

In 1969 all major program benefits were indexed to inflation, but in 1975 a new and complex system of indexation treated different programs in different ways. On average, however, the new system overindexed pensions, increasing them 1.1 to 1.2 percent for every 1.0 percent increase in prices. As a result, average pensions in the general program increased from less than 30.0 percent to more than 60.0 percent of per capita net national income between 1955 and 1980.

Overly generous benefits make up only one part of the current crisis confronting the Italian social security system. The other involves demographic trends and population aging, as in all other countries studied in this book. In 1955 the ratio of

---

*These programs include the general scheme, programs for the self-employed, welfare pensions, programs for state (central government) employees, for public enterprise employees, and for those employed by local authorities, as well as other minor schemes.

insured workers to pensions* in the general program was 3.62; in 1980 it had fallen to 1.41, and it is expected to decline further to 1.32 in the year 2000—which is vastly lower than in other countries. During this same period the median age of the Italian population is expected to continue climbing into the next century, with the percentage of the elderly (those over age 60) growing from 17.30 percent to 21.60 percent over the next two decades.

To finance these increasing benefits, the payroll tax rate in the general scheme rose from 9.0 to 24.2 percent between 1955 and 1980. But despite these increases, contributions are still not sufficient to cover benefits. Huge deficits, financed by increasing the national debt, have emerged in both the employee scheme and that of the self-employed, and future trends are still gloomier. Either the payroll tax rate will have to rise to fantastic heights—over 30.0 percent—or the yearly deficits will increase in absolute terms and as a percentage of GNP.

Net national saving declined from 20 percent of net national income in the 1960s to 15 percent in the 1970s, because an increasing share of private sector savings are absorbed by public sector deficits. Roughly half of the deficits are accounted for by social security.

In the general program there is an earnings test which allows pensions up to 250,000 lire (about $200 per month; L = $0.0008 U.S. as of 1 July 1981), regardless of a worker's earnings, but confiscates pensions above that amount. There are also guaranteed minimum benefits for eligible pensioners under all the major schemes. These two facts give many an incentive to switch from the official to the underground economy, which is thriving.

The Italian system redistributes a great deal of money in a haphazard fashion. It favors women, who live longer and can retire earlier. It favors the self-employed, who enjoy a more

---

*The word "pensions" refers to the number of legal pensions, not to the number of pensioners, whose precise number is unknown. The number of pensioners is somewhat smaller than the number of pensions, because some pensioners are receiving more than one pension.

favorable ratio of contributions to benefits than do employees. And it favors public employees whose benefit formula is more generous than that of private employees and who are not subject to a qualifying age. Much of this redistribution is regressive.

There is only one way to straighten out the redistributional maze and to reduce expenditure to a level which voters will be willing to finance: that is to reduce those benefits which are unnecessarily high and which offer higher than average returns on contributions. Ideally, this would involve the creation of a unified social insurance system with higher qualifying ages.

The development of social security legislation in recent decades seems to have followed the principle that every pensioner is a person in need, that whatever measure taxes active workers (or increases government deficits) in order to raise the income of pensioners is good. It is high time to review this principle and to restrain at least the growth of benefits. Although politicians on many sides realize the utmost urgency of such a reform, the shortsighted day-to-day tactics of the political parties have so far prevented adoption of a long-term strategy.

The first programs—those for state and local employees—date from the end of the nineteenth century or the first decade of the twentieth. The general program followed in 1919, and the three principal schemes for self-employed workers, in various years between 1957 and 1966.[1] (Table 1 describes the principal programs.) Despite their differences, the major programs do have two common elements. First, they provide benefits which appear to be very generous as compared with payroll taxes paid and with those of other countries; second, most of them suffer chronic and growing deficits. Table 2 reveals the extent of this generosity. The general scheme is one of the most liberal programs in the world, but the conditions offered to state employees are even more lavish. If they enter the civil service at 20 years of age, a man of 40 and a woman of 35 (if married *or* with children) become eligible for a pension which may run as high as 60 percent of their last respective salaries.

Besides old-age pensions, disability pensions have been granted so easily in the past twenty years that in December

Table 1
Insured Workers and Pensioners, 31 December 1980
(millions of people)

Scheme	Workers	Pensioners
Private employees		
"General" scheme	12.0	8.400
Others	0.6	0.220
Public employees		
State	1.8	0.800
Local authorities	1.2	0.300
Public enterprises	0.3	0.250
Self-employed		
Farmers	1.8	1.980
Craftsmen	1.7	0.570
Tradesmen	1.6	0.530
Others	0.4	0.100
Public assistance		
(Welfare) pensions	—	0.675
Total	21.4	13.825

Sources: For general scheme, principal self-employed schemes, welfare pensions: Italy 1979*b*; for public employees and minor programs (altogether adding to more than thirty): Italy 1979*a* (author's extrapolations).

1980 there were as many disability as old-age pensions within the general scheme and 3.7 times as many disability as old-age pensions within the farmers' scheme. These figures are really extraordinary, even after accounting for the statistical convention of continuing to regard as disability pensions those payments made after a beneficiary has crossed the age threshold for retirement pensions. Widows and—since 1978, in the name of sex equality—widowers are entitled to survivors' pensions regardless of age, working position, or dependents.

It is the financing of this generosity in the general scheme that requires a payroll tax of 24.2 percent to be applied to earnings, with no ceiling.

Table 2

Some Data on Contributions and Benefits

Scheme	Payroll tax rate (%)		Old-age pensions		
	Employer	Employee	Age	Contribution period	Amount
"General" scheme	17.05	7.15	M 60 F 55	15 years	2% of average salary of last 3 years for every year of contribution (max. 80%). Guaranteed floor equal to 30% of current minimum wage of industrial workers.
State employees	—	7.00	M/F 65	15 years or 20 without age limit (reduced to 15 for married women)	Roughly 2.35% of last salary for every year of contribution (max. 94%). Guaranteed floor equal to about 60% of. minimum wage of public employees.
Self-employed (craftsmen, tradesmen, farmers)	Fixed amount (about $430/yr. in 1980, but much less up to 1978; reduced figures for farmers)		M 65 F 60	15 years	Fixed amount (about $2,000 a year in 1980).

Source: Text of relevant laws and calculations thereon. Italian liras have been converted into dollars at a rate of 1,000 liras to a dollar. No ceiling exists on taxable earnings nor on state pensions. General scheme pensions are subject to a ceiling of roughly $10,000 a year, soon to be raised to $15,000 a year.

SHORT- AND LONG-TERM FINANCIAL PERFORMANCE

The state and public enterprise schemes have no separate accounting; the Treasury simply withdraws the payroll tax from salaries and hands out benefits when due. The private employees' general scheme was established on a funded basis, but when the real value of its reserves (state bonds) vanished owing to wartime (1940-1945) inflation, it turned to pay-as-you-go.

From the beginning, the main schemes for the self-employed handed out benefits to the retired (or close to retiring) generation and were therefore unable to build up a reserve. Pay-as-you-go was their obligated choice. Only the local authorities' scheme still works on a funded basis. Table 3 gives an overview of the development of the general scheme and the self-employed schemes over the last three decades.[2]

Table 3

Some Data on the Principal Schemes

(A)
General Private Employees Scheme

Year	Insured workers (millions)	Pensions[a] (millions)	Payroll tax rate (no ceiling)	Minimum pension ("floor")	Average old-age pension[b]
1950	10.5	1.8	5.00	—	0.29
1955	10.5	2.9	9.00	0.26	0.39
1960	10.5	4.2	15.75	0.35	0.45
1965	12.0	5.3	19.40	0.44	0.57
1970	12.0	6.4	19.40	0.37	0.54
1975	12.0	7.8	20.60	0.43	0.62
1980	12.0	8.5	24.20	0.42	0.61

(B)

Self-Employed Schemes

Year	Insured workers (millions)	Pensions[a] (millions)	Yearly contribution (U.S. $)[c]	Average pension[b]
1950	—	—	—	—
1955	—	—	—	—
1960	8.4	0.9	12	0.19
1965	6.0	1.3	24	0.27
1970	6.1	2.2	24	0.27
1975	5.3	3.0	90	0.40
1980	5.0	3.0	430	0.36

Sources: Istituto Nazionale della Providenza Sociale, various yearly reports; net national income from national accounts; author's calculations.

[a]"Pensions" refers to the number of legal pensions, not to the number of pensioners, whose precise number is unknown. The number of pensioners is somewhat smaller than the number of pensions, because some pensioners are receiving more than one pension.

[b]Percentages of per capita net national income (NNI).

[c]At current rate of exchange.

The history of the general scheme from 1950 to 1980 shows the typical behavior pattern of pay-as-you-go; a much more rapid increase in the number of pensioners than in the number of workers (369 percent as against 14 percent) has led to a five-fold increase in the payroll tax rate. This also applies to the schemes for the self-employed, where the number of insured workers is actually decreasing because of the diminishing proportion of farmers in the work force. Between 1960 and 1980 the yearly contribution (as a fixed amount per person, not as a proportion of income), originally set at a ridiculously low level, has been multiplied by ten in real terms.

But this is not all. A small financial support from the Treasury was originally envisaged for both the general and the self-employed schemes. But aggregate revenue (contributions plus planned Treasury support) has been insufficient to pay for aggregate benefits since the early 1960s for farmers, since the early 1970s for the other self-employed (craftsmen and trades-men), and since the late 1970s for the general scheme. A deficit thus has emerged not only in the long run, when the present values of future revenues and expenditures are compared, but also in the short run, in terms of current flows.[3] Altogether, aggregated deficits in all retirement programs equaled about 30 percent of total program costs in 1980, and that deficit has been financed simply by absorption into the national debt.

What happened? Over a built-in bias which tends to push pay-as-you-go pension systems too far (see Browning 1975), Italy has superimposed a strong dose of Mediterranean light-heartedness. Whenever a new scheme has been introduced, or when both contributions and benefits of the existing schemes have been raised, government, Parliament, and public opinion alike have fallen prey to myopia. Forecasts have seldom seen more than five years, and contributions have been set so as to balance with benefits within this comparatively short period after taking account of the planned support from the Treasury.

Even when original forecasts have not been too optimistic (which they sometimes *have* been), as far as they went the balance has been upset in the following period. Demographic trends, as almost everywhere else, have moved against the balance by raising the number of pensioners more rapidly than the number of workers. Overliberal disability tests have made matters worse.

So have legislated improvements in the benefits formulae, including overindexation. From time to time, up to 1969, Par-liament increased money benefits roughly in step with consu-mer prices. In 1969 automatic indexation to the consumer price index was introduced, and in 1975 a new and cumbersome system of indexation tied some benefits more than propor-tionally to consumer prices, some just proportionally, and some less than proportionally. On average, however, the elastic-ity of pensions (in money terms) to consumer prices is more than one: a 1.0 percent increase in prices leads to a 1.1 to 1.2 percent increase in pensions. As mentioned earlier, the average old-age pension in the general scheme thus increased from less than 30.0 percent to more than 60.0 percent of per capita net national income (NNI) between 1955 and 1980; in the self-employed scheme, the corresponding figure roughly doubled between 1960 and 1980.

What now? While the current deficit in all the main schemes is a permanent nightmare for the Treasury minister, no comfort may be drawn from looking into the more distant future since demographic trends are no more obliging than those in most other countries. On the revenue side, the rate of payroll tax seems to leave little room for any further increases, let alone for an increase as large as was decreed between 1950 and 1980. Recourse to general revenue is not advisable in a country which already ranks so high in terms of the ratio of the state deficit to GNP (see the following section). As will be seen in the final section, the only solution is a radical reformulation of the rules determining entitlement to benefits and their levels.

Table 4

Age Distribution of Italy's Population
(percentage points)

Age	1951	1961	1971	1981	1991	2001
0-14	26.1	24.5	24.4	22.2	18.0	18.7
15-59	61.7	61.6	58.9	60.5	62.0	59.7
60 and over	12.2	13.9	16.7	17.3	20.0	21.6

Source: Italy 1978, supplement no. 10 (for 1951-1981); Italy 1980 (for 1991-2001).

IMPACT OF THE SOCIAL SECURITY SYSTEM ON SAVING AND INVESTMENT*

The literature concerning the impact on saving of a pay-as-you-go social security system usually and implicitly assumes

*The section on saving and investment was written by Dr. Emanuela Guglielmino, Faculty of Economics, University of Turin.

that aggregate contributions match aggregate benefits. Since
the early 1970s in Italy, however, benefits have exceeded contributions. Attempts to quantify the impact of social security
on saving and investment—even when they rely on sophis-
ticated econometric estimates—are subject to dispute, as every
reader of the Feldstein/Munnell/Barro et al. controversy
knows. No such estimates have been made for Italy, nor is the
present writer in a position to fill the gap.

The available figures are nevertheless sufficient to outline a
broad picture. Table 5 shows net saving (as percentage of net
national income) in the aggregate and by sector in the last two
decades.[4] While from 1961 to 1970 the government maintained
a surplus, it spent itself into deficit from 1971 to 1980.[5] The
government's aggregate deficit, moreover, has been greater
than that of the social security system; the latter's deficit, in
other words, has not been paid—even partly—by general taxation and has simply flowed into the aggregate deficit, thereby
increasing the public debt.

Table 5

Net Saving, National and by Sector
(percentages of net national income)

Year	Families	Firms	General government	(Of which: OASDI deficit)	Net national
1961-65	14.5	1.8	3.6	(—0.3)	19.9
1966-70	14.6	2.5	1.4	(—1.7)	18.5
1961-70	14.6	2.2	2.5	(—1.0)	19.2
1971-75	21.1	—1.2	—4.6	(—2.6)	15.3
1976	23.1	—2.4	—6.6	(—2.9)	14.1
1977	23.1	—4.6.	—6.4	(—2.9)	14.1
1978	21.8		—6.7	(—3.0)	15.1
1979	22.3		—6.2	(—2.7)	16.1
1971-79	20.5		—5.4	(—2.7)	15.1

Source: Author's calculation on the basis of national accounts and social security reports.

A comparison of the 1961-1970 with the 1971-1980 period shows that:

• In the second decade, net national saving was much lower. The overall government deficit (to which social security contributed roughly one-half) has therefore been consistently accompanied by a reduction in national saving.

• Yet this reduction (—4.1 percent of NNI between 1961-1970 and 1971-1980) has been lower, in absolute terms, than the reduction in the government's saving (—7.9 percent) because family saving has increased, partly offsetting the reduced government saving.

This increase is striking, because it runs counter to the usual, Feldstein-type argument that expansion of pay-as-you-go social security protection reduces personal saving. It is therefore of interest to see whether offsetting forces have been operating.

Partial explanation for increased family saving may be found in the drastic reduction of the larger (especially public)[6] firms' profits which took place in the 1970s; as firms' saving declined and the share of labor income grew, family saving increased. But even after merging families and firms, total private saving increased in the 1971-1980 decade as compared with 1961-1970 (20.5 percent against 16.8 percent). The rise in family saving and the less-pronounced rise in private saving may be understood in terms of two different, though not mutually exclusive, lines of thought.

First, the increased government deficit, mainly due to the increase in social security and other transfers, has *ceteris paribus* increased family disposable income and thus family saving. To accept this conclusion, it is not necessary to adhere to a Barro-type model of behavior which implies that pensioners wish to offset the effect of social security on their offspring. It is sufficient to postulate that pensioners have a greater than zero marginal propensity to save[7]—an inclination particularly likely for those pensioners (formerly self-employed) whose pension schemes were introduced only in the

1958-1966 period. Since they formerly could not reckon on social security, they had accumulated personal savings and/or private insurance, and when the public pension came—almost as a windfall—their consumption behavior was not revised upwards to absorb the full amount of the new benefits.

The second line of thought concerns the interrelation between inflation, erosion of the real value of outstanding public debt (even after taking account of accrued interest) and therefore of private financial wealth and family saving. It is a problem common to most countries in the Organization for Economic Cooperation and Development, but it is particularly pronounced in Italy.

When comparing United Nations statistics for the 1960s with the (much more inflationary) 1970s, the United States, France, Germany, Italy, Japan, and the United Kingdom all show (within a reduced rate of net national saving on GNP) relative increases in family saving combined with relative declines in the saving of firms and government (see Ferri-Szegö 1980, pp. 498-99).[8] The reason for this increased private saving may be that families pursue a wealth target in real terms. Therefore, whenever inflation exceeds the average rate of interest on the public debt, it destroys part of the previously accumulated private (financial) wealth[9]—which families in turn try to offset by increased saving (see Howard 1978; Bank of England 1977, pp. 27-28: Caranza 1980, n. 1).

To sum up, the Italian social security system affects saving and investment in at least four different, although related, ways:

• Contributions, which are seen as "social security saving" by active workers, reduce private saving while financing current transfer expenditures.
• Since contributions are insufficient to pay benefits, the resulting deficit must be covered by increasing the public debt, which is held in part by family saving (e.g., through purchase of government bonds or payments into savings deposits). Therefore, part of family saving is channeled to

current transfer expenditure by the families themselves or by the banks buying the public debt.

• Social security is thus responsible for a consistent share of the huge financial needs of the government. The desire to neutralize (at least partly) the consequences of issuing money and Treasury bills and to ease the absorption of longer-term public debt during the 1970s led to a severe monetary policy, both quantitatively and in its discrimination against private recourse to the banking system. This behavior has also put a brake on investment.

• Inflation, which results—at least, in part—from the government deficit, implicitly taxes the owners of financial wealth by reducing the real value of the public debt and induces them to increase their saving.

While the first three items operate against saving and investment, the fourth appears to favor them. But apart from the fact that the strength of the latter has not been sufficient to offset the other influences, aggregate saving has, in fact, decreased (see table 5). It is sad to realize that social security has a positive effect on saving only insofar as it contributes—through the government deficit—to that most inequitable tax, inflation, thereby destroying previously accumulated private financial wealth; i.e., it creates *in*security.

INFLUENCE ON EMPLOYMENT

The work test

The work test operates rather inconsistently. Under the general scheme, a pension is paid within a given limit (the equivalent of up to ca. $200 per month) and "confiscated" above it; this pension amount is paid regardless of a worker's earnings. A public employee must resign to get his pension, but does not lose any fraction of it if he afterwards accepts a job in the private sector or in the free professions. No work test applies to the self-employed, nor to agricultural or domestic employees.

In addition, a basic minimum or "floor" benefit is guaranteed, even if earnings would not support it under the standard formula. This minimum works also as a "ceiling" for those whose earnings are below a certain level. Therefore, after reaching the minimum contribution period under the general scheme (fifteen years for old-age pensions and five years for disability pensions), people with discontinuous and low-wage working records have no incentive to work and to pay contributions for additional years. Their pension will not rise above the floor, and the implicit return of additional contributions will be zero.

This legal framework will produce not so much a diminished as a distorted supply of labor. Pensioners, both of the disability type (but often not really disabled) and of the old-age type (but often not really old), look for jobs in the "black labor" market. The same is also true of future pensioners, who know their pension will not rise above the "floor" even after additional contributions.

The existence of a diffused "unofficial" or "underground" Italian economy was first observed at the beginning of the 1970s. This sector is made up of the self-employed and of very small firms, along with part of the activity (and labor force) of larger firms; it became evident as the fall in official labor participation rates became too rapid to be realistic. The hypothesis thus appeared that there existed a considerable amount of "underground" employment which escaped the tax collectors and the official statistics. A number of field tests, performed in different regions, have supported this hypothesis, so the Central Institute of Statistics has recently changed its method for collecting labor market data. The official participation rate is now 39 percent, which is much more realistic than the 36 percent emerging from the old series.

This unofficial sector is in part due to entrepreneurs' efforts to escape labor legislation (minimum wages, constraints on dismissals, limits to overtime, safety rules) and taxes on profits and turnover. Attempts to operate underground are likely to be more successful in peripheral areas where labor is abundant

and trade unions weak. But both the work test and the zero
marginal return in circumstances discussed above surely encourage workers and entrepreneurs to cooperate in pursuing their
mutual interest underground.

The labor/capital choice

Scholars in Italy and abroad think that social security has
little or no influence on the labor/capital choice.[10] If one
adheres to the prevailing view that both the employer's and the
employee's share of the payroll tax are ultimately shifted to the
employee, the cost of labor to the employer—and therefore his
choice between labor and capital—is unaffected. But even if
the cost of labor is raised by the tax, the same conclusion
applies, since this indicates an increase also in the cost of capital goods.

The choice between labor and capital appears to be more influenced by the general state of the labor market and by legal
or contractual constraints on working hours, overtime, mobility, dismissals, etc.—and, of course, by the availability and
cost of finance—than by the existence and level of payroll
taxes.

EQUITY AND REDISTRIBUTION

When the general scheme was introduced in 1919, it promised actuarial equity on an individual basis, though with
some corrections in favor of the lower-paid workers. Increasingly important exceptions to the rule were made after the war
(1940-1945), when increased money benefits, strongly re-
quested by pensioners, were made—not proportionally, but
principally in the form of equal *absolute* increases for every-
body. In 1952 a minimum was established for benefits. This
"floor" is important, since it now applies to almost two-thirds
of the pensions.

In 1968-1969 a new formula for calculating benefits was
introduced into the general scheme. The old formula was based

on contributions (payroll tax) paid over the entire working life;
the new formula—previously in force only for public employees—is based on the average salary of the last three years
only (for public employees, of the last month).

The main distributional features of the Italian system are
summarized below, assuming that the employer's share of the
payroll tax is entirely shifted onto workers.

Within generations

(a) Farm employees have always paid—within the general
scheme—preferential payroll tax rates while enjoying benefits close to or equal to the rest of the general scheme.

(b) After one year as an employee, he (or more often, she)
who has left the labor force can continue to pay contributions and thereby acquire the corresponding entitlement to
benefits. These voluntary contributions were trifling until
1978; they still are very low, so that they offer—thanks to
the "floor"—a generous rate of return.

(c) In the general scheme (see table 2), women get their old-
age pension at age 55 (as against age 60 for men) and, of
course, they live longer. In contrast, women have a lower
probability than men of leaving survivors (spouse or children under age). But this fact does not offset the preferential
treatment enjoyed by women, implied in receiving pensions
over longer retirement periods.

(d) Contributions (in fixed yearly amounts) made by the
self-employed were kept extremely low until 1978 (see table
3), and then gradually raised. But even today the relation
between benefits (pinned to a "floor") and contributions is
much more favorable for the self-employed than for general
employed workers.

(e) Calculating benefits on the basis of the last three years'
(or last month's) salary, while the payroll tax was paid
yearly on current salary, is a great bonus for those in dynamic careers. In smaller firms, where a personal agreement
between employer and employee is easy, this formula also

creates a powerful incentive to underreport the salary of every year except the last three (which entails a saving of payroll tax with no loss of benefits) and to overgenerous increases in the last three years' salary.

(f) Other redistributional impacts, already mentioned, include the generosity of disability pensions in the "general" and self-employed schemes, and the ability of state employees to claim so-called old-age pensions after twenty years' contribution, fifteen for married women or unmarried mothers. A similar rule applies to employees of the local authority, but with five more years' contribution in both cases—with the years spent as a university student before entering the administration (state or local authority) counted as working years.

Between generations

When the "general" scheme was established in 1919, workers less than ten years from pension age (at that time, 65 years) got special treatment—although they were required to work at least five more years before being entitled to benefits calculated by the standard formula. They were therefore not required to contribute for the normal ten-year qualifying period and were favored in having the standard formula apply to their shorter working careers.

In 1952, when the minimum "floor" was introduced for benefits, the period-of-contribution requirement was reestablished and was raised to fifteen years. But only in 1962 did this requirement become fully effective. In the meantime, the older generation could receive the minimum benefit even with a shorter contribution history.

The self-employed got the best treatment of all. When the schemes for farmers, craftsmen, and tradesmen were introduced (1957-1966), the elderly population was granted the right to benefits (pinned to a "floor") after only one year of contribution.

Comment

The Italian social security system was born in 1919 in the spirit of actuarial equity, slightly amended in favor of the lower-paid workers and thus in the direction of social adequacy. Later developments (1950-1980) brought many departures from actuarial equity. The question now is this: Has the current system approached further social adequacy, or is it just a senseless maze?

This writer's feeling is that the huge redistribution of income (aggregate benefits amount to some 12 percent of GNP) implied in our pension system sometimes is merely random and sometimes runs quite opposite to any acceptable definition of social adequacy.

Random redistribution includes the following:

• Former employees who voluntarily continue paying contributions at preferential rates may be housewives in large and poor families, but also may be typists who have given up working to marry their boss or, more generally, women belonging to well-to-do families.
• When millions of disability pensioners who are not really disabled live in the poorer and less-industrialized regions of the country, their pensions may be interpreted as an unemployment dole in disguise. But if they live in more-industrialized regions, they often actually work in the "black labor" market (i.e., they not only receive undue benefits, but also escape both payroll and general taxation).
• Overindexing or underindexing of benefits for inflation leads some pensioners to an improvement—and others to a worsening—of their relative positions. One is struck by the contradiction of a political establishment which repeats at every occasion its concern about inflation, but which at the same time delegates to the future—unwanted and unknown—inflation rate the task of determining income redistribution among pensioners.

The following involve regressive redistribution:

• The preferential treatment (both of the first generation and in general) of the self-employed favors craftsmen, tradesmen, and farmers, whose average income—except for farmers living in the mountainous and southern regions—is higher than that of the industrial workers.

• Public employees who resign at 35 or even 45 years of age are generally either women whose families enjoy an above-average standard of living or men who may exploit in private professions the experience they acquired in the civil service. In neither case do they seem to deserve a gift from the over-all community.

• The formula connecting benefits to the last years' salary favors, with a higher than average rate of return, those with dynamic careers and with higher final incomes.

Finally, it should be added that insofar as the government deficit is at least partly responsible for inflation, the social security system, by contributing to that deficit, is also partly responsible for the implicit tax that inflation imposes on the owners of financial wealth. As small savers are much less able than big savers to differentiate their assets and much more likely to keep them wholly or mainly in financial form, the inequity of this method of financing benefits is no small sin of the social security system.

SUMMARY AND CONCLUSION

The most distinctive features of the Italian pension system are haphazard redistribution and huge deficits. The redistributional maze stems from the large number of separate schemes unconnected by a systematic and unifying plan. The implicit rate of return on contributions varies between different schemes and between different individual situations within the same scheme, with no logical connection with needs. Higher than average rates of return are sometimes unrelated to need, and are sometimes systematically correlated with higher, not lower, incomes.

The huge deficits show that the average citizen is not willing to foot the full bill of the system directly. Workers and firms alike resist further increases in payroll tax rates. This is because full shifting of the tax onto workers may only occur over the long run, while firms may be forced to bear increases in the short run, at least partly. Voters (and tax evaders) object to further increases in general taxation. But unless real resources can be called forth through bigger aggregate demand—a Keynesian phenomenon which is neither normal nor permanent— the deficits must ultimately be borne by someone, if only through the blind forces of inflation.

As I have said, the only acceptable way simultaneously to cure the redistributional maze and to reduce aggregate benefits to reasonable levels is to reduce increases of further benefits by reducing higher than average implicit returns on contributions where need is not shown. Some healthy steps in this direction have recently been taken. The self-employed contributions, so desperately low until 1978, have been raised considerably— though to a level that remains insufficient. Voluntary contributions have also been revised upward, and disability tests, because of new legal definitions and more severe medical examinations, are no longer so easy to pass.

More basic reforms are envisaged in several bills submitted by the government to Parliament in recent years (1978-1980). These reforms include not only a new and more restrictive treatment of disability, of voluntary contributions, and of contributions due by agricultural employees, but also—most important—a drive towards a unified social insurance system and a higher pension age for both private and public employees. Unfortunately, these bills have met strong resistance by those groups which feel most hit, and almost every group has found protection from a policital party (there are nine in Parliament).

The reforms have been stalemated and worse; Parliament has picked out those parts of the government bill which will actually lead to larger expenditures (such as an increase of the minimum "floors" and more frequent indexation of benefits to inflation). The problem is acute, because more severe rules on, say, age of retirement or disability requirements, even if rapidly approved, could only be applied to new pensions awarded from now onwards. Their impact on the total "stock" of existing pensions, and therefore on total expenditures, would be felt only gradually over time.

Stronger medicine should immediately apply to the whole stock—for instance, by reducing adjustments for inflation. But pensioners are apt to regard as an inviolable right their present real benefits and the overindexing rules underlying their benefits. Thus pensioners—millions of them (see table 1)—would strongly resist such a reform, while the diffused benefit to the rest of the population would not, typically, generate sufficient support for the reform to offset the opposition.

The outlook is therefore rather bleak. The Italian social security system is not quite social because it redistributes income almost at random; it is not quite secure, because it is not entirely financed by taxes consciously voted but relies on a inflation-creating deficit. Because of deficit financing, the harmful impacts of the pay-as-you-go method on capital formation are particularly strong. Yet the courage has not yet been found to reform the system fundamentally. Such courage will only be found when the government, Parliament, and especially the voters realize that just as there are no free meals, neither are there free pensions.

5

NORIYUKI TAKAYAMA

Japan

Financial performance of the KNH. Funded and unfunded financing. Savings, investment, and employment. Income redistribution. Funded reserves and the retirement age. Problems and solutions. Mandating private pensions.

Japan has eight public pension programs covering different sectors of the population.* The earliest plan was established in 1890; the most recent, in 1961. Although each system has its own contribution and benefit structure, the seven systems for employees are similar, operating largely like funded insurance systems, with about 10 percent contributions and with benefits equal to about 45 percent of past annual earnings in real terms.[1]

Since the Japanese population is now relatively young and few pensioners are receiving benefits in relation to the numbers of workers paying in, benefits in 1978 for all compulsory government programs amounted to only 3.76 percent of gross national product (GNP). That number, however, will grow substantially in the decades ahead.

This chapter will focus on the public pension system for private enterprise employees, KNH (*Kosei-Nenkin-Hoken*), which has the widest coverage of the eight systems and is still growing.

The KNH provides old-age pensions with a two-tiered structure: a flat-rate minimum, and a supplement on top of the minimum related to contributions. Both are financed as a largely funded system, with 20 percent of program costs paid by contributions from general revenues. The funded part of the system is financed by a payroll tax—10.6 percent on men and

*I am grateful to Lawrence Chickering for his many helpful suggestions, and also to Akiyoshi Horiuchi, Tsuneo Ishikawa, Shuzo Mishimura, Masahiro Okuno, and Jean-Jacques Rosa for their valuable comments.

8.9 percent on women, split equally between employee and employer—levied on incomes up to a very high ceiling of 410,000 yen per month ($1,804 U.S. at an exchange rate of Y = 0.0044 as of 1 July 1981).

The KNH pays old-age benefits to women at age 55 and to men at age 60 on a sliding scale, depending on income—with 42 percent of past real wages paid to the richest pensioners and more than 100 percent to the poorest.[2] Twenty years of contribution are required for full benefits, and benefits are legally indexed to inflation. In addition, Parliament has increased benefits every five years to reflect real income growth in the economy, though these increases have been discriminatory. Besides old-age pensions, the KNH also provides survivors' pensions, orphans' benefits, and disability benefits.

Japan is now experiencing a very rapid aging of its population, and the ratio of workers to retirees in the KNH is expected to decline from 11.5 in 1976 to 2.7 in 2000 and 1.6 in 2025. In a pay-as-you-go system, declining demographics combined with a decline in expected economic growth rates would create very serious funding problems. Fortunately for Japan, however, the KNH has accumulated a considerable funded reserve which, with normal rates of return, would avoid any funding problem even at the worst of the demographic cycle. Unlike most other countries in this book, Japan should be protected against adverse demographics.

Unfortunately, it enjoys no such protection because of government investment policies which place the program reserves in instruments that pay a below-market return. In real terms, the reserves have been receiving negative returns; and unless this policy is reversed in the near future, the KNH will be forced to abandon its funded system and convert to pay-as-you-go, as other countries have done. If so, future tax rates would have to rise substantially to maintain currently legislated benefits.

If anything, the current social security system probably increases total saving in Japan because of its accumulation of a funded reserve. However, if the system is forced gradually to liquidate the reserves to pay benefits, the impact on the Japanese capital stock could be very different.

The KNH has an earnings test which reduces benefits by a complicated formula for pensioners aged 60 to 64 and by a lesser amount for those 65 and above. At present, it is unlikely the earnings test affects many employment decisions because of a special problem the elderly have in finding employment in the Japanese labor markets except at wages which are very substantially lower than the wages they were paid in their normal occupations. Unless this problem is somehow solved, employment will continue to be a problem for the elderly—whether the earnings test remains in force or is eliminated.

Apart from normal intragenerational transfers from rich to poor employees, problems of equity arise in the use of general revenues—supported by low-income taxpayers—to support high-income pensioners. The largest equity problem, however, occurs between generations. Present beneficiaries of the KNH receive an excessive intergenerational transfer, which is more than the minimum income given by public assistance. On the other hand, in the near future young workers will be forced to pay far greater real contributions to receive fewer transfers.

There is a simple solution to the future funding problems of the Japanese social security systems, and that solution is simply to invest the funded reserves in the private capital markets at positive real rates of return. This simple reform, combined with continuation of the general revenue subsidy, would eliminate the long-term funding problem suffered by most other countries studied in this volume. Barring that, Japan will begin to travel down the unhappy road that is so well known elsewhere.

BACKGROUND AND STRUCTURE OF THE KNH

The public pension system for private employees—the KNH—dates from 1942, with its present form established in 1954. With the introduction of an index-linked benefit formula, the KNH raised the old-age benefit drastically in 1973, paying 60 percent of the past average annual earnings *without* bonus (about 45 percent *with* bonus) in real terms. This percentage was for a "model" retiree with an average wage earned for all contributing years. On the sliding scale, benefits vary depending on income, from 42 percent for the richest pensioner to more than 100 percent for the poorest. Total outlays for the flat-rate minimum in 1973 equaled slightly more than 50 percent of total old-age benefits.

To finance this system, the KNH imposes a payroll tax on male employees equal to 10.6 percent of the regular monthly earnings *without* bonus (Hyojun-Hosyu-Getsugaku [HHG]), and 8.9 percent on women. These tax rates are split equally between employees and their employers up to the high maximum of 410,000 yen ($1,804 U.S.) per month in 1980.[3] The payroll tax rate was initially set at 6.4 percent in 1942 and in 1944 was raised to 11.0 percent; it was reduced to 3.0 percent in 1948, but since 1954 the relatively low rate has been reviewed at least every five years to make the system's financing more actuarially sound.

Contributions from the beginning have been accumulated in a reserve fund and deposited in the Fund Administration Branch to be invested in forming social overhead capital for construction of highways, railways, bridges, airports, and other public projects. The government, however, sets the interest rate earned by the fund at a little more than 6 percent, substantially below the high rates of return on private investment. This implies a subsidy by the pension system to other recipients of that capital, aggravating the future financing problem of the KNH.

Although the KNH currently enjoys a surplus of revenues over benefits, 20 percent of current benefits are covered by transfers from general revenues. Even with this 20 percent subsidy, the current system is not actuarially sound, in part because of the below-market return paid on the fund. If it were, of course—and assuming continuation of the 20 percent subsidy—changing demographics would present no financing problem in the future.

SHORT- AND LONG-TERM FINANCIAL PERFORMANCE

Japan is still a very young country which experienced rapid economic growth until the early 1970s. If the KNH had had a pay-as-you-go system, with current workers paying taxes to finance pensions for current retirees, the tax rate for male employees in 1976 could have been reduced to only 3.9 percent instead of the actual rate of 9.1 percent (or 9.8 percent, taking the government subsidy into account), which supports a partially funded system.

Both demographic and economic factors in the future will probably impose great stress on this system, and may even force liquidation of the capital fund. This is because the KNH now faces a rapid aging in its population resulting from increases in the numbers of those covered, increasing life expectancies, and declining fertility rates. For example, between 1947 and 1960 the total fertility rate (children per family) fell from 4.5 to 2.0; it stabilized around 2.1 until 1970, and then declined to 1.8 in 1978. At the same time, life expectancy for men who reach age 65 rose from ten years in 1947 to fourteen years in 1978, and for women, from twelve to seventeen years in the same time periods. Table 1 shows that in 1976 there were 11.5 workers paying contributions for every person receiving a pension; in 1980 that number fell to 8.2 workers; in 2025 the equivalent number will be only 1.6 workers paying for each retiree! To put the point another way, the ratio of retirees to workers in the KNH will grow over the next forty years from one to eight in 1980 to five to eight in 2020. This 400 percent rise in the retiree-to-worker ratio is equivalent to 4.1 percent annual aging of the KNH population. Note that table 1 optimistically assumes that the total fertility rate will remain unchanged at 2.1 in the future, above the current rate of 1.8. This implies that the actual figures will be worse than those projected here.

In the second place, future wage-rate growth in the KNH is likely to decline from levels of 10 percent real annual growth, achieved in the period of 1955-1975, to probably below 4 percent. This declining rate of economic growth will almost certainly reduce over time real KNH revenues in relation to benefit payments.

Table 1

Population Aging in the KNH[a]

Fiscal year	Contributors[b] (1)	Beneficiaries[b] (2)	(1)/(2) (3)
1976	24.6	2.1	11.5
1980	25.4	3.1	8.2
1990	29.4	6.7	4.4
2000	31.4	11.5	2.7
2015	31.4	18.2	1.7
2025	31.4	20.1	1.6

Source: Japan 1976, p. 22.

[a]Figures assume that the total fertility rate will remain unchanged at 2.1 in the projected future—which is above the current (1978) rate of 1.8.

[b]Contributors and beneficiaries are in millions.

Pay-as-you-go financing. It is extremely fortunate that Japan has a partially funded social security system, and not a fully unfunded one—as in many other countries—which depends on collection of taxes on current workers to pay benefits for current retirees. In a fully unfunded system, the demographic and economic trends just mentioned would force enormous increases in KNH tax rates (see table 2). According to official estimates which assume no future real wage-rate increases, in a fully unfunded system for which current tax rates would be 3.9 percent, rates would have to rise to more than 30.0 percent to pay anticipated benefits in the next thirty years (see case A in table 2). With 1.0 or 2.0 percent growth, which seems more realistic, tax rates would still have to rise substantially, though not as much (see cases B and C).

Table 2

Estimated Tax Rates in a Fully Pay-As-You-Go
Financing of the KNH[a]

Fiscal year	Benefits[b] (1)			Tax base[b] (2)			Tax rate[c] (1)/(2)		
	A	B	C	A	B	C	A	B	C
1976	7	7	7	177	177	177	3.9%	3.9%	3.9%
1980	11	11	11	193	201	209	5.6	5.5	5.5
1990	26	28	30	232	267	306	12.2	10.4	9.8
2000	50	57	66	258	328	415	19.6	17.6	15.9
2015	88	109	140	269	397	582	32.8	27.7	24.1
2025	101	132	183	271	441	715	37.1	29.9	25.6

Key: A = no wage rate increase in real terms.
     B = 1 percent annual increase of wage rate in real terms.
     C = 2 percent annual increase of wage rate in real terms.

Source: Japan 1976, p. 27; B and C cases are given by author.

[a]The 1980 ceiling is 410,000 yen (about $1,804 U.S.) per month, and is assumed here to be indexed to wage increases. It is thus extremely high.

[b]Benefits and tax base are estimated at 1976 prices in U.S. billion dollars ($ = 200 yen). The tax base is a total sum of wage income regularly paid (i.e., HHGs).

[c]The tax rate takes account of the 20 percent government subsidy.

Funded financing. As we have seen, Japan has a partially funded system which provides a more substantial cushion against the deteriorating demographic condition of our social security system. Demographic changes can exert no direct influences on a fully funded pension system. What really matters in a funded system is the real rate of interest.

To get actuarially sound contribution rates to ensure pension benefits equal to 60.0 percent of real earnings during contribution years, consider a man who begins to work at age 20 and dies at 80. Table 3 shows actuarially sound rates of contribution for two retirement ages—60 and 65—in a fully funded program under several real rates of return on investment and assuming no real wage-rate increases.[4] It is clear from the table

Table 3

**Actuarially Sound Contribution Rates in
a Fully Funded Pension System**

Real annual rate of return on investment	Contribution rate	
	(1)[a]	(2)[a]
0	20.0	30.0
1	14.7	22.2
2	10.7	16.2
3	7.7	11.8
4	5.5	8.6
5	3.9	6.2
6	2.7	4.5
7	1.9	3.2

[a](1) and (2) assume retirement ages of 65 and 60, respectively.

that different real rates of return will produce enormously different rates of contribution. To support currently legislated benefits, for example, at the present retirement age of 60 and with a 2.0 percent real interest rate, the payroll tax rate applied to today's high wage ceiling would have to rise from the current rate of 10.6 to 16.2 percent. At zero real interest rate, however, payroll taxes would have to rise to 30.0 percent—or nearly triple—to support the same benefits.

Increasing the retirement age from 60 to 65 will greatly mitigate, if not eliminate, the future problem. If the normal pension age were increased to 65 in a fully funded system with 2.0 percent real interest, we could continue paying current benefits by maintaining the present contribution rate of 10.6 percent. If the interest rate were zero, however, the rate would have to be 20.0 percent, almost double the current rate.

Obviously, these figures are very conditional. What table 3 can tell is not the estimated future financial performances of the KNH in a fully funded system, but merely the sound rates of contribution for an individual in a fictitious setting. To estimate actuarially sound contribution rates which would ensure currently legislated benefits, we should estimate for a representative individual, while taking into account both the low past rates of contribution (less than 10 percent for the past thirty years) and the regulated below-market rates of return paid on the fund. The picture, in fact, is worse than that painted in table 3, particularly because in recent years the KNH has been receiving negative real interest—less than zero percent—on its funded reserves.. As a result, it seems extremely likely that contribution rates will have to be increased to more than those shown in table 3.

Despite these problems, since the KNH is still in its start-up phase and does not yet have major current burdens, we can reduce the required rise in contribution rates by maintaining the 20 percent general revenue subsidy, together with 1 or 2 percent real annual wage-rate growth.

Alternative financing systems compared. In comparing pay-as-you-go and funded systems, the essential question involves comparing the probabilities of either of two trends. Is Japan more likely to earn 2 percent real annual return on investment, which would sustain the current, funded social security system; or to achieve annual real wage growth exceeding 6 percent, which would support equivalent real revenue growth in an unfunded system? It is likely that future real annual wage increases will not exceed 2 percent, but real annual rates of return on investment will probably be positive—that is, exceeding zero percent. This implies that it would not pay to finance the future KNH on a fully pay-as-you-go basis.

The future. To make the most of funded financing, it is obviously important to get as large a real return as possible paid on the funded reserve. Nevertheless, the mandatory deposit of the KNH reserves has yielded a negative return because of a regulated, below-market rate of interest. The funded reserve of the KNH amounted to 2.1 trillion yen ($9.24 billion U.S.) in March 1979, but the KNH has been forced not to make the best use of it.

Unless the policy which regulates below-market returns is changed, it will probably force abandonment of the partially funded feature of the present KNH, substituting in its place a largely pay-as-you-go system. Increasing resort to pay-as-you-go financing will also force rapid increases in contribution rates to more than 20 percent in the next thirty years.

Young workers entering the KNH in the near future will discover sooner or later that they can buy annuities in the private market at lower cost than what they must pay to the public system for equivalent benefits. At that point, young people will become disaffected with the burden they face, and they might well refuse to pay tax increases exceeding, say, 20 percent. If this happens, the present KNH will collapse. The future of this system does not seem very bright.

INFLUENCE ON SAVINGS AND INVESTMENT

The question of whether the public pension system discourages personal saving and private investment has been a large question for Japanese policymakers and business leaders, who are concerned about possible adverse effects on capital formation and, therefore, on future economic growth. While the question remains open even for economists,[5] the public pension system can affect personal saving in two principal ways.

Tax effect. The tax effect assumes that, for a large portion of the population, private saving and the payroll tax for old-age support are almost perfect substitutes. If this is true, it follows that the greater the payroll tax, the less people will currently save. Whether or not reduced private saving reduces total economic saving depends on alternative financing bases. With unfunded pay-as-you-go financing, adverse effects on total savings will result unless additional government saving is forthcoming.[6] However, to the extent a system is funded, involving government saving, reductions in personal saving will be offset. Pay-as-you-go systems may have unintended influence on savings and investment; funded systems do not.

Arguments about these impacts on saving have limited relevance for Japan. Among others, the motives for saving are much more complex than simply for retirement. Younger people in Japan are apt to be too shortsighted to save for retirement in these rapidly changing times. Rather, they save primarily for ill health and unforseen expenses, or to buy their own houses. Only those aged 50 and over seriously begin saving for retirement. With a relatively young population, as in both past and present Japan, increasing public pensions thus will reduce private saving only slightly.

The most important point, however, is that since Japan has partially funded systems, its public pension plans probably have increased rather than reduced total savings. With little saving motives for retirement, the funded financing, in fact, has served to force saving and thus to increase the total amount saved. Forced saving would have allowed increased government investments to Japanese social overhead capital, contributing to higher productivity.

In summary, past experience in Japan suggests there have been no adverse tax effects on savings, although this conclusion should be understood only as a theory which still needs empirical verification.

Wealth effect. Another conceivable adverse effect comes from the prospect of receiving benefits with a much higher present value than taxes paid, which is very common in start-up phases of public pension systems. Several outcomes are possible. The expected bonus may reduce contributors' saving for their own retirement, or it may induce those receiving pensions to save more; they may not spend all of their bonuses. The latter will lead to bigger bequests, which might enable younger generations to save less. If reduced saving of younger generations exceeds increased saving by the elderly, net saving will decline.

Such possibilities are based on the assumption that younger people have rational expectations and are saving primarily for retirement. As suggested, however, I doubt that these motives explain why younger people in Japan save, while such motives certainly explain why beneficiaries of public pensions would probably increase their saving, as it is reasonable to expect they would. Through the wealth effect, in fact, public pensions might actually increase total personal saving in Japan rather than decrease it. But no empirical evidence on this influence is yet available.[7]

Summary. Though different factors will exert conflicting influences, the net effect of Japan's funded public pensions is likely to have increased total savings by increasing government capital formation and inducing additional saving by the elderly. We can imagine unintended adverse effects on savings and investment only when a public pension system is financed on a pay-as-you-go basis with dominant personal saving motives for retirement. Without strong empirical findings, however, we cannot draw definitive conclusions.

INFLUENCE ON EMPLOYMENT

The KNH has a work earnings test which, in 1980, reduced basic benefits to eligible employees aged 60-64 by 20 percent for the monthly regular earnings from 1,000 to 94,000 yen, by 50 percent from 95,000 to 129,000 yen, and by 80 percent from 130,000 to 154,000 yen, and eliminated benefits altogether above that amount. At age 65 they can receive full benefits up to 154,000 yen ($678 U.S.), and 80 percent above that amount.

On the effects of the work test, Boskin (1977, pp. 6-8) has shown—using income-leisure choice theory—that the work test can induce earlier retirement.[8] However, earlier retirement, if any, would be of minor importance to Japan, since the number of beneficiaries at present is small.

Regarding future effects, a prior problem exists in the Japanese labor market: the demand for labor. In general, the market is extremely thin for older workers and few jobs are available for them at prevailing wages. For social, cultural, and other reasons, the value of workers above age 55 is considered to be rather low. Mandatory retirement agreements between employers and unions, which maintained retirement at 55, codified this fact. Faced with the rapid aging of the population, a number of companies recently increased the mandatory retirement age to 60. Nevertheless, jobs still are difficult to find for people between 55 and 60 because of the continuing bias against hiring the elderly. After the retirement age—and for many, even before it—older people can only find jobs if they are willing to take substantial wage cuts. Since many are unwilling to do that, they elect instead to be unemployed. The extent of this problem is indicated by the fact that the effective demand/supply ratio of age 55 and over has been pegged at an astonishingly low level from 0.1 to 0.2 over the past twenty years.

The government since 1976 has tried to impose a legal employment quota, requiring companies and institutions—both public and private—to employ at least 6 percent of their employees from those aged 55 and older. As the requirement has no penalties, however, nearly 60 percent of the companies failed to reach this level in 1978. Despite the general desire of older workers to continue working as long as possible, the market for them is very thin. The problem will grow much more serious in the future as the population continues to age.

EQUITY AND REDISTRIBUTION

The Japanese social security system—like those of other countries—incorporates both an insurance objective, creating earned entitlements for those who contribute, and a redistributive objective, assisting people with lower incomes. Almost all systems confront difficulties in trying to incorporate these conflicting objectives into the same programs, and the Japanese system is no exception.

Intragenerational transfers

The old-age benefits of the KNH consist of a flat-rate minimum and an earnings-related pension. The former entails a progressive transfer of wealth from rich to poor employees within given generations.

On the other hand, the payroll tax used primarily to finance transfer payments is regressive for several reasons. Brittain (1972, pp. 37-38) has shown that the employer and employee contributions of that tax will make no difference as far as their effects on resource allocation are concerned.[9] Discussions only on the employer portion of the payroll tax thus will suffice. First, the tax—as Musgrave (1959, pp. 306-9) has concluded—in the short run will be partly shifted forward to consumers, who on average have disproportionately lower incomes. Second, increasing employers' contributions and therefore prices will decrease demand and therefore output resulting in reduced employment opportunities. It will also increase the cost of labor, hitting unskilled low-wage workers hardest. In this respect, the burdens of the payroll tax are partly shifted to wage-earners. Third, the payroll tax is not imposed on earnings above the ceiling, nor on property income.

Another regressive effect results from the use of general revenues to finance 20 percent of current benefits. To the extent benefits are paid by this transfer, it is not clear why general taxpayers should subsidize high-income pensioners.

Payroll tax rates vary between male and female employees—10.6 percent for men and 8.9 percent for women in 1980—but they receive the same basic benefits. This implies a transfer from male to female employees for which the reasons are unclear, to say the least. The problem of transfers from men to women is aggravated, moreover, by the fact that women become eligible for benefits earlier (age 55, versus 60 for men), and live longer after retirement (twenty-six years, versus eighteen for men in 1978).

Intergenerational transfers

Every public pension system involves a transfer from younger, richer generations to older, poorer men. The value of these transfers equals the discounted sum of expected benefits minus contributions plus interest. The size of these transfers is considerable, as the following examples will show. A newly qualified pensioner making average earnings during his working years would have an accumulated wealth of 1.7 million yen at 1978 prices. Given the remaining life expectancy of a man aged 60, the discounted present value of expected benefits for him and his dependent wife would be 14.2 million yen. The system thus would transfer some 12.5 million yen ($55,000 U.S.) to him, or 88 percent of his benefits. [10]

These numbers assume that the dependent wife has not participated voluntarily in the public pension system for the nonemployed. If she had, the couple would have an accumulated earned entitlement of 1.8 million yen in 1978, while their total benefits would be increased to 17.3 million yen with increased transfer of 15.5 million yen at 1978 prices, or almost 90 percent of total benefits.

Most self-employed people are farmers, craftsmen, and tradesmen, whose income is generally less than that of employees. A newly qualified, self-employed couple of 65—for purposes of comparison—would have an accumulated wealth of 0.2 million yen in 1978 as against total benefits of 5.9 million yen and a transfer of 5.7 million yen ($25,080 U.S.), or 97 percent. While it is true that self-employed couples get proportionately greater transfers than the employed couples, they get considerably less in absolute terms, which implies another regressivity. [11] The voluntary participation of employees' dependent wives in the public pension system for the nonemployed would exacerbate the problem still more.

Present beneficiaries of the KNH receive a transfer from current working generations amounting on average to 88 percent of total benefits. They might have a plausible claim for this, having made great contributions to the country's rapid economic growth for more than twenty years, both by their high saving rate and by having large families. But the absolute amount of that transfer seems excessive; an elderly couple under public assistance in 1978 received 82,000 yen ($361 U.S.) monthly, and a newly qualified pensioner whose wife had not participated voluntarily in the other public pension program would receive an average monthly welfare transfer of 92,000 yen.

Intergenerational equity would require equal contributions between different age cohorts as long as the number of children per family remains unchanged. As already shown, however—without a change in investment policies—the present KNH presupposes rapidly increasing contributions for the next forty years to maintain current benefit levels.[12]

In summary, the current KNH involves several regressive transfers within generations as well as a rapid rise in the real contributions of younger workers in the near future, which may create tensions between the generations.

TOWARD A SOLUTION

Reduce the long-term funding problem

I have shown in this chapter that the most serious problem with the present KNH is the future long-term financial crisis. To reduce this problem, we must either raise revenues or reduce benefits, or both.

Earn market rates of interest. The funded reserves of the KNH have been forced to earn negative interest in real terms, while private pensions are enjoying real annual returns of 2.0 or 3.0 percent by investing in the private market. If the KNH earned market rates of interest, the system could avoid the impending funding crisis without increasing the contribution rate of 10.6 percent.

Officials say that the rapid aging of the population should require increased contribution rates in the near future, but this is disingenuous. The government's practice of managing the funded reserves at negative rates of return is the main threat to the integrity of the KNH. This practice should be reformed by allowing the KNH reserves to earn market rates.

The government will inevitably oppose this move, since the mandatory deposits have enabled it to borrow at below-market cost. Contributors to the KNH, however, may soon realize how their investments are being mismanaged, and until their funded reserves are allowed to earn market returns, they may become resistant to paying further tax increases.

Maintain economic growth. Maintaining economic growth is a critical factor, given severe limits on opportunities to raise contribution rates. By increasing the personal income on which taxes are levied, revenues can be increased even with a constant tax rate. Increasing the incentives for saving and investment in order to ensure continuing productivity growth is important to encourage economic growth.[13]

Raise the normal pension age. Later retirement will not only increase revenues but will reduce benefits. In 1980 the authorities proposed to lift the normal pension age gradually from 60 to 65. Despite resistance from interest groups, this makes sense, especially since the elderly have a great deal to contribute to the work force and life expectancies are rising. Earlier retirement with partial benefits also should be available. At the same time, the work-earning test might be abolished, since it tends to induce earlier retirement.

Enforce a legal employment quota with penalties. Once we raise the retirement age, however, we run into the problem of the scarcity of jobs for the elderly, due principally to continuing prejudice against hiring older workers. One way to solve this problem will be to enforce a legal employment quota for the elderly *with penalties* so severe as to motivate every company to employ the quota. Although they are very resourceful in avoiding regulations, employers would soon begin to find proper jobs for older workers or to increase their productivity.

Such an employment quota would consequently promote an increase in mandatory retirement ages.

Limit transfers to a minimum. With relatively few people receiving benefits, it was easy (as well as politically irresistible) for the KNH to pay on average very large transfers from working generations to retirees. With the growth in numbers of retirees and resulting future funding problems, it may be advisable to reduce to a minimum transfers to the elderly—perhaps to the minimum given to low-income people by public assistance. The political prospects for this, however, are uncertain.

Attain equitable transfers

In considering options for reform, it is important to assign policy instruments which are appropriate to the system's two rather different goals—redistribution and insurance—while separating these functions as much as possible. The transfer goal could be accomplished by paying a flat-rate minimum pension out of general revenues, while the insurance goal was achieved by mandating purchase of private pensions. This general scheme, of course, implies phasing out the payroll tax altogether.

Pay a common flat-rate minimum. A flate-rate minimum transfer should be paid to the elderly, and all participants—men and women, employees and the self-employed, and public and private employees—should be treated equally. The minimum should also be paid out regardless of contributions. Household economies of scale make it possible to pay an old couple less than twice the benefits of a single person. Moreover, both recipients should have reached the retirement age—say, 65. The law should also be changed to eliminate differentials in the normal pension age between men and women and between employees and the self-employed.

Finance the minimum through general revenues. The minimum benefit can be regarded as part of society's general concern for the elderly,[14] and thus should be paid for out of

general revenues. As Patton (1977, p. 165) points out, a major
problem with paying transfers from revenues raised through a
payroll tax is that the payroll tax encourages people to think
they are paying not for transfers, but for earned entitlements to
pension benefits when they retire. Since people think they are
paying in for their own benefit, much resistance to tax increases is thus lost—and with it much of the discipline on program costs—as transfers increase. Shifting from the payroll tax
to general revenues would restore some of this discipline as the
legislature was forced to consider social security transfers in
relation to other priorities of social spending. Such a transfer
would also eliminate some regressiveness in reliance on the
payroll tax.

In 1977 the Japanese Council on Social Security Systems
proposed that a flat-rate pension should be financed through a
new, earmarked, value-added tax. Earmarking, however, has
the effect of insulating a tax from competition from other, pos-
sibly more valuable uses. Earmarking a value-added tax, therefore, would allow the legislature to avoid judging transfer
benefits in relation to other public priorities. General-revenue
financing would force such judgments and comparisons.

PRESERVE EARNED ENTITLEMENTS
BY MANDATING PRIVATE PENSIONS

To meet the insurance goal, it would suffice for the government simply to mandate that people purchase private pensions,
group or individual. Mandating would reduce sales costs.
Moreover, by maximizing the insurance pool, mandatory insurance would increase the reliability of probability estimates,
allowing further reductions in premiums.[15]

No transfers from general revenues should be involved here,
since each private pension should be financed on an actuarially
sound basis. Full funding would avoid possible adverse effects
on savings and investment. Private pensions, moreover, would
enjoy a higher rate of return on investment than the govern-

ment currently allows for the KNH, and private pensions would also maintain intergenerationally neutral burdens. Needless to say, we would also enjoy a wider choice.[16]

In devising an overall public pension strategy to meet the insurance goal, there is nothing wrong with relying in part on private insurance. It is very important that people who can support themselves should not be allowed to behave irresponsibly and to impose costs on others, especially on future generations who have no political influence today.

Japan is still young now, and her payroll tax rate is moderate in comparison with other industrial countries. Although the current picture is bright, the present public pension system should be radically reformed as soon as possible to minimize long-term financial burdens caused by the aging of the Japanese population. While the political temptation is strong to delay reform, the longer the delay in addressing the long-term financial problems, the more serious those problems will become.

6

INGEMAR STÅHL

Sweden

Basic and supplementary pension systems. Saving disincentives. Three approaches to transfers. Proposals for change. The use of accounting units. Housing benefits, health care, retirement homes. Negotiated pension schemes. Social security and the capital market. Unemployment. Future problems.

The Swedish social security system has several tiers. A basic pension scheme gives equal pensions to all retired people; a compulsory supplementary program pays pensions related to previous income; and there are free health services and a number of local government services. Private pension plans play an insignificant role.

The basic pension is a flat-rate benefit which is not related to prior income and which is formally financed on a pay-as-you-go basis by a payroll tax of 8.4 percent. There is no ceiling on incomes on which the tax is levied, and the tax is paid entirely by the employer. This basic program pays 15,300 kroner (SEK [$3,014 U.S. at an exchange rate of SEK = $0.197 U.S. as of 1 July 1981]) to single persons at age 65 and 25,000 SEK ($4,925 U.S.) to married couples. Lesser amounts can be paid at age 62, and a complex formula indexes all pensions to inflation. Total spending on basic pensions equaled 6.2 percent of gross national product (GNP)* in 1979-1980.

The supplementary pension system (ATP) is also financed on a pay-as-you-go basis by an earmarked payroll tax of 12.25 percent—this, too, paid entirely by the employer—levied on incomes between a floor of 16,100 SEK ($3,171) and a ceiling of 120,750 SEK ($23,788). Proposals are currently before Parliament to abolish the ceiling.

*For Sweden, gross domestic product (GDP) is the same as gross national product (GNP).

Combined benefits for the basic and supplementary pension programs, when the system reaches maturity in 1990, will be calculated at 60 percent of the fifteen best earning years over a thirty-year qualification period. Until then, the qualification period is being gradually increased from twenty years. Benefits are indexed to inflation, though this indexing does not cover all items in the consumer price index.

Although the ATP itself has no funded reserves, the program was established with a system of forced saving in a central government fund in which were invested most taxes collected in the first years of the program. As a result, the present fund of about 150 billion SEK is very large in relation to the Swedish capital market, which has 320 billion SEK in assets owned by households, including private insurance.

The Swedish social security system also includes substantial additional benefits not provided to the elderly by other countries. It provides housing benefits based on need, benefits which can be as high as 9,000 SEK ($1,773) per year, along with programs at the county level to provide almost complete health care services. For the very old (those over age 75), the expense is considerable, particularly in hospital costs. More than 50.0 percent of the health care resources in Sweden thus are spent on the 16.0 percent of the population over 65 years of age. Since out-of-pocket health care costs are minimal, this very large redistribution to the elderly through medical care amounts to about 5.0 percent of GNP, compared with some 6.0 percent for the basic pension program and 3.3 percent for the supplementary program.

Since the ATP system has not yet reached maturity, the ratio of workers paying into the system to retirees receiving benefits is still rather high, particularly in relation to that of other countries studied in this book. Nevertheless, Sweden is subject to the same general population aging that afflicts other countries, and the ratio of workers to retirees is thus expected to decline from 6.84 in 1980 to 3.44 in 2020.[1] Of the current 12.25 percent ATP tax rate, 9.50 percent goes to support current pensions and the balance accumulates in the capital fund. Support of future benefits will depend on future real wage growth. At 3.00 percent growth, which is probably unrealistically high, the tax rate would have to increase to 24.20 percent in 2020 to support currently legislated benefits; at no wage growth, the rate would have to rise to 34.40 percent. Such increases themselves, of course, would produce harmful effects on the economy. Either way, the current system cannot continue without modification toward the reduction of benefits.

High taxes, combined with pay-as-you-go systems, discourage saving in Sweden except for investment in owner-occupied houses, for which significant tax breaks are available. The Parliament, recognizing the added disincentives to saving implicit in creating the pay-as-you-go supplementary ATP, established along with it the forced saving scheme.

Since the special additions to the basic pension and housing benefits are reduced automatically when a pensioner earns outside income, even in the lowest income brackets people may face marginal tax rates equaling 63 percent. It is thus not surprising that labor force participation of males has declined noticeably in recent years. The system has almost certainly increased female participation before retirement, since women can increase their retirement benefits disproportionately by an extra year of work.

In addition to the normal intergenerational transfers implied by pay-as-you-go systems, the Swedish social security system also favors beneficiaries with fluctuating earnings records—such as professionals—over people with steadier long-term earnings.

The political forces supporting the Swedish social security system are similar to those in other countries. Benefits concentrated on current retirees and costs diffused over many taxpayers (including many future taxpayers who cannot vote at present) account for the pressure to increase benefits beyond the system's ability to support them responsibly. The long-term problem will have to be faced, however, and—as in other countries—the sooner it is faced, the easier it will be to find long-term solutions.

THE BASIC APPROACHES TO SOCIAL SECURITY

In principle, there are three broad approaches for transferring resources from working generations to those who are not working.

• A family system in which there is an implicit contract between generations: parents take care of their children, and children, in turn, later take care of their aged parents. This primitive system was probably sufficient in a preindustrial age and could be described as a pay-as-you-go system within the family.

• A market-oriented system in which the individual starts life by borrowing to pay for his needs during childhood and adolescence, then repays the debt and accumulates insurance for retirement. In the real world, there is little "borrowing" during childhood and adolescence, and children's consumption is mainly financed by their parents.

• A social welfare system which redistributes wealth between the generations through public transfers. Such a system may include different forms of children's allowances, or subsidies in king such as "free" day-care centers, schools, and for the retired, subsidized pensions and nursing care.

The Swedish system has been marked by a rapid change from the family to the social welfare approach, in line with Sweden's evolution from a mainly agricultural economy into a highly developed industrial one. The largest programs have been mentioned: a basic pension scheme which gives equal pensions to all retired people, a compulsory supplementary pension scheme which provides a pension related to previous income, "free" health services, and a number of local government services. Private pension plans are of little importance.

All these public programs are financed on a pay-as-you-go basis. This reduced incentives for private saving over the life cycle, increased marginal tax rates, and created a need for enforced government saving to compensate for the loss of private saving.

THE BASIC PENSION (FOLKPENSION)

The basic minimum pension is a flat-rate benefit, independent of prior income, formally financed on a pay-as-you-go basis by a payroll tax of 8.4 percent paid by the employer, with no ceiling on the earnings on which the tax is levied.

The first tax-financed general pension system was introduced in 1913 and provided basic pensions for all citizens above 67 years of age as well as disability pensions of the same amount. This system has gradually been extended to include pensions to survivors, housing benefits, and a special means-based supplement. At present, the basic old-age pension for a single person is 15,300 SEK ($3,014) and 25,000 SEK for married couples. In 1979-1980 total spending on basic pensions amounted to 6.2 percent of GNP.

The basic pension is independent of previous and present income and is expressed as a percentage of an index-linked accounting unit (one accounting unit being approximately 16,100 SEK at present) which was created to express pensions and other social welfare programs in terms of constant purchasing value. For a single person, the basic pension is 0.95 accounting units, and for a married couple, 1.55. Persons receiving only the basic pension also get a special addition equal to 0.40 accounting units, which means that the present guaranteed level for a single pensioner is 1.35 accounting units.

Prior to 1981 the accounting unit was linked to the general consumer price index. In autumn 1980 it was decided that the index should not reflect changes in indirect taxes, consumer price subsidies, and energy prices. This decision was a part of the government's crisis package, and is expected to reduce the nominal value of future pensions one or two percentage points below the levels that the original index would have yielded.

Since the payroll tax is not earmarked and there is no special budget for the basic pension, for all practical purposes the basic pension is financed out of general revenue on a pay-as-you-go basis.

THE GOVERNMENT'S SUPPLEMENTARY
PENSION (ATP) SCHEMES

For a long time the basic pension was the mainstay of the social security system. In addition, employees of central and local governments had supplementary pensions, established to maintain their pension level at a certain fraction of their last income. Although not formally indexed, these government pensions have generally kept pace with inflation. Pensions for government employees were—and still are—financed out of current income, with no accumulated capital fund.

In the private sector, most white-collar workers negotiated comprehensive schemes which, by the 1950s, guaranteed them pensions related to their previous working income. These schemes are still mainly funded, with premiums calculated on an actuarial basis. A few blue-collar workers, principally in government enterprises such as the state railway, were covered by such schemes, but most—like farmers and some self-employed people—had only the basic pension and social welfare assistance.

After more than twenty years of Social Democratic government, the party's core constituencies were still unprotected by one of the major features of the modern welfare state. Nevertheless, the trade unions were not interested in following the same path as white-collar workers (i.e., by negotiating with employers) and looked instead for a solution through government legislation. Inflation in the early 1950s substantially reduced pension-fund values. Interest rates were held down to 3 percent at a time when inflation in some years reached 20 percent. Pressure for some kind of indexed benefits ensured that change was inevitable.

A number of special commission reports on change included proposals to introduce indexed loans in the capital market. Finally, in a 1957 referendum, the electorate was asked to choose between three alternatives:

• A compulsory supplementary government pension scheme guaranteeing real values of pensions in relation to previous income. This was supported by the Labor party and the trade unions (including white-collar workers), and it got 46 percent of the votes.

• A further expansion of the basic pension scheme, combined with individual supplementary pensions (with government guarantees of real value). This was the most egalitarian option; it provided an equal basic pension for everyone and was financed by proportional or progressive taxes. Its main support came from the Farmers' party, and it got only 15 percent of the votes.

• Group pension plans, similar to existing plans for white-collar workers but with institutional changes in the capital market allowing for index-linked bonds or similar devices. This plan was supported by industry and employers and by the Liberal and Conservative parties, and got 35 percent of the votes.

After some years of political turmoil and new elections, the first proposal was enacted in 1951 by a margin of one vote—from a Liberal defector.

The ATP system pays a pension that, combined with the basic pension, gives the beneficiary a pension level equal to 60 percent of his or her average income during the best fifteen working years. When the program reaches maturity, thirty years of qualification will be necessary to be eligible for a full pension; in the meantime, the first generation entering the system in 1960 could qualify with only twenty years' contributions, so the first full pensions were paid in 1980. The number of years to qualify will gradually increase until 1990, when the thirty-year limit will be reached.

Each individual's annual wage income is recorded in terms of accounting units, as mentioned; income history is stored in the pension files in units of constant purchasing power. Therefore—except for the recent manipulation of the index—the system is inflation-proof. All wage income below 7.5 accounting units (at present, 120,750 SEK) creates an entitlement to future supplementary pension rights.

Clearly, the scheme has no actuarial base. The program features substantial redistributions within and between generations.

Financing the ATP scheme

The supplementary pension is financed by an earmarked payroll tax paid entirely by employers on all wage income between 16,100 SEK (1.0 unit) and 120,750 SEK (7.5 accounting units). The payroll tax started in 1960 at a level of 3.00 percent, rose to 7.50 percent in 1965, to 10.00 percent in 1970, and is now 12.25 percent. There is at present a proposal before parliament to abolish the upper ceiling on the tax, but pension rights will still be limited to wage income below 120,750 SEK.

The present ATP scheme is a compromise between complete funding and pay-as-you-go. It was obvious that the introduction of a compulsory pay-as-you-go system would decrease savings in the funded group plans. To compensate for this, and perhaps in an attempt to increase savings in a welfare society which has low incentives for private saving, the supplementary pension system included forced investment in a central government fund, and most taxes collected during the first few years were invested in this fund.

At present the system has reached a stage (see table 1) in which the real value of the fund is no longer growing. As more and more persons acquire full pension rights, payments from the fund are increasing and interest income is becoming insufficient to cover paid pensions. With an annual 10.0 percent inflation rate, the excess of income over expenditure is just enough to preserve the real value of the fund. It should also be observed that the annual yield for the fund in 1979 was just 8.5 percent because most of the fund is invested in low-yield government bonds or in semigovernmental mortgage institutions. The real rate of interest on the investments for a number of years has been negative.

The present fund of about 150 billion SEK is large when compared with the total Swedish capital market. The fund compares with total financial assets owned by households

Table 1

Development of the Supplementary Pension Scheme (ATP)
(million SEK)

	1960	1965	1970	1975	1979
Total income	483	3,410	8,360	15,564	30,897
Taxes	470	2,905	6,100	10,746	19,347
Interest	13	505	2,260	5,818	11,550
Pensions paid	—	153	1,165	5,008	15,077
Fund increase (savings)	478	3,204	7,075	11,390	15,448
Capital value					
of fund investments	480	10,644	39,000	88,560	146,914

(including private insurance) amounting to 320 billion SEK; household debts amount to 245 billion SEK. Two aspects of the fund will be discussed later: the economic and political implications of a large fund with a nonprofit-oriented incentive structure, and the size of the fund compared with some alternatives.

Housing benefits

Pensioners are entitled to municipal housing benefits paid by local authorities and financed through a local income tax along with transfers from the central government. For pensioners without a supplementary pension or other extra income, the housing benefit covers a substantial part of housing costs. The maximum benefit for a single person is about 9,000 SEK per year. Total expenditure on housing benefits was 9 billion SEK in 1979.

The housing benefit is income related, and is reduced by a third when income increases above the basic pension. This means that supplementary pensions, like earned income and wealth, are taxed at a marginal rate of at least 33 percent.

OTHER GOVERNMENT PROGRAMS

The redistributive effects of pension programs should not be discussed in isolation from programs which offer benefits in kind. In Sweden, these include health care, which is almost completely provided by the government and is financed by a proportional income tax at the county level. In addition, local welfare programs offer special homes and other help for the retired. Money pension levels are determined simultaneously with benefit levels for other programs as well as with the rules for taxing pensions. The programs can be regarded as communicating vessels: assuming a more or less constant budget level, a rise in out-of-pocket costs of health care sooner or later affects political decisions regarding pension levels.

Apart from this connection between them, all of these programs together form the Swedish social security system, broadly understood. In some countries, many of these programs are combined under a single umbrella program. In Sweden, they are separate but complementary parts of a whole.

The overriding political question here is how much the present working generation is willing to decrease its own consumption in order to support the older nonworking generation. There is no single answer; only an intricate web of different rules, with individual pressure groups favoring some programs and fighting others. Decisions are made at different levels of government. These complications make it especially important to look at the system from the outside and from a longer-term perspective.

Modern health care focuses predominantly on old people, especially on the very old. Table 2 shows the relationship between age and hospital use. It is striking how fast use increases for the very old. Another remarkable feature is the decrease in the average number of hospital days per person between 1964 and 1976 for all age groups except those over 75. A tentative conclusion may be that improvements in the productivity of health care—resulting from improved technology and a tendency to produce more intensive care during a shorter hospital stay—are the main factors behing the decline in use. Improved general health may also be part of the explanation. Increasing costs per hospital day thus are partly offset by shorter periods of stay.

Table 2

Hospital Days per Inhabitant in Different Age Groups 1964 and 1976

Age	Somatic care		Psychiatric care	
	1964	1976	1964	1976
0- 4	1.2	0.9	0.0	0.0
5-14	0.5	0.3	0.0	0.0
15-24	1.1	0.6	0.4	0.3
25-34	1.2	0.6	0.9	0.7
35-44	1.3	0.9	1.3	0.9
45-54	1.9	1.4	1.8	1.1
55-64	2.8	2.4	2.5	1.6
65-69	4.8	4.0	NA[a]	NA
70 and over	10.9	14.2	NA	NA
65-74[b]	NA	5.2	3.1	3.0
75 and over[b]	NA	19.6	4.8	8.2

Source: Patientstatistik (Uppsalaregionen).

[a]NA = not available.

[b]These additional figures are provided to show numbers for psychiatric care, which numbers are not available in the age groups given in the main table.

For the very old, there has been a considerable increase in hospital use. Technological advances have made it possible for older people to undergo surgery and complicated medical procedures, and an increased availability of resources facilitates treatment of patients for whom the resulting improvement is marginal. There is also evidence of a considerable shift of care from homes and other community institutions to the health care system. Changing economic incentives and the increased participation of women in the labor force may be important contributing factors. A large number of elderly patients, such as those with senile dementia or terminal cancer, require care and not cure. Mortality statistics show that increased hospitalization has not increased life expectancy of the elderly. From analysis of Swedish data, it seems reasonable to conclude that more than 50 percent of the health care resources are spent on the 16 percent of the population above 65 years of age (for hospital days, the share is 65 percent for the group above 65 years, but outpatient treatments are more evenly distributed). With almost 10 percent of gross domestic product (GDP) used in the health care sector and with insignificant out-of-pocket costs, this means that almost 5 percent of GDP is transferred to the elderly as a subsidy in kind.

These numbers suggest that the transfer of real resources through the tax-financed health care system is larger than the transfers through the supplementary pension system (which amounted to 3.3 percent of GDP in 1979) and roughly the same size as those transferred through the basic pension system (6.0 percent, but including disability pensions, early retirement resulting from long-term unemployment, and family pensions).

Health care services in Sweden are provided by the county, a political level between central and local government with its own political assemblies and administration. There are twenty-six counties in all. Other social services for the elderly are provided by local governments. These services had a production value of about 8 billion SEK in 1979, representing a further transfer of 1.7 percent of GDP.

Within the context of this chapter it is not possible to identify all those services designed primarily to benefit the elderly. Besides homes for the retired and direct assistance, there are a number of programs such as subsidized transport and special rates for a vast array of local government services. The figure indicated here for total transfer to the elderly is probably an underestimate.

NEGOTIATED PENSION SYSTEMS

The different government programs so far covered are typically pay-as-you-go, although the ATP—which includes a "fund"—is a form of forced saving. Since pension levels are set independently of the pension fund's yield, the ATP should be regarded as part of the total government budget. (Future tax levels may be based on the yield, but there is no direct relationship, since the tax is a component in the government's overall economic strategy.)

There are two different types of negotiated pension schemes. The first is for central and local government employees, all of whom work on a pay-as-you-go basis. The scheme's main beneficiaries are those who are not entitled to a full supplementary pension because they fall short of the required qualification time; the government pays the difference between the ATP pension and the negotiated pension level. Almost all negotiated group pension plans are now coordinated in this way with the ATP system.

The private schemes are generally either funded or of a premium-reserve type. The main institution in this category is the Svenska Personal-Pensions-kassan (SPP), founded in 1917 to provide pensions for white-collar workers. The role of this organization changed drastically in 1960 when the ATP was introduced, and its principal purpose now is to provide supplementary pensions to the ATP schemes—which means pensions for incomes above the ATP maximum or pensions for people who retire before age 65.[2]

Although the SPP is formally a private pension scheme, it now resembles a public program, privately administered by trade unions and the employers' federation. The fees and premiums are generally a fixed percentage of an individual's salary; thus they resemble a private payroll tax. To safeguard indexed pensions for those who have already retired, the present working generation pays an extra "real value guarantee premium", which makes the SPP nothing more than a pay-as-you-go system.

The premiums in the SPP system can either be paid into the SPP fund or be retained and reinvested within the private companies (with pensions guaranteed by SPP, which receives an extra insurance premium for offering the guarantee). The present level of pensions paid out by SPP is 1.0 billion SEK per year. Premiums received amount to 3.2 billion SEK, and the total fund has a value of 27.0 billion SEK. Most of the fund is invested in bonds and in other nominal securities. Only a small fraction—1.0 billion SEK—is invested in Swedish equities.

In addition to the SPP, including enterprise-based pension systems, there is a small market in which other private insurance companies offer pension and life insurance.

THE LONG-TERM FINANCING PROBLEM

The ATP system has not yet reached its maturity. In 1980 only persons born in 1915 received their full pensions, and in coming years each new generation will receive full pensions as it reaches the required thirty qualification years. Table 3 gives

Table 3

Ratio of Workers to ATP Pensioners

Year	Active population (millions)	ATP pensioners[a] (millions)	Ratio
1977	5.015	0.611	8.21
1980	5.017	0.734	6.84
1985	5.077	0.893	5.69
1990	5.102	1.051	4.85
1995	5.134	1.122	4.58
2000	5.189	1.141	4.55
2005	5.199	1.164	4.47
2010	5.132	1.260	4.07
2015	5.039	1.401	3.60
2020	4.998	1.452	3.44

[a]Excluding those on survivors' and disability pensions.

some projections on the relation between the working population and the number of pensioners. The future is thus a perspective of a stable or slightly declining working population and an increasing number of pensioners entitled to ATP's pensions, with the ratio of workers to retirees expected to decline from 6.84 in 1980 to 3.44 in 2020. The payroll taxes necessary to finance benefits will rise correspondingly. With the present payroll tax of 12.25 percent, some forced savings in the ATP fund is still possible. The ratio of taxable wage income (with the present floor and ceiling) to pensions paid out in 1980 was 9.50 percent, which would be the payroll tax in a complete pay-as-you-go system without any accumulation in the capital fund.

With the population projection shown in table 3 and assuming, for groups between 16 and 65 years of age, a constant labor-market participation rate for men (90 percent) and an increasing rate for women (from 73 percent in 1980 to 81 percent in 2020), it is possible to calculate the necessary payroll tax for a system without funding. Since future tax rates depend, however, on the growth rate of real wages, table 4 presents two alternatives, one assuming a real growth rate of 3 percent, the other assuming no growth.

Given currently legislated pension formulae, a low increase in future real wage growth would increase the ratio between pensions and average earnings above the current ratio of 60 percent. A low economic growth rate for at least the next decade could result from the modest growth of the Swedish economy in recent years and the necessity in increase corporate profitability to cope with trade deficit problems.

On the other hand, increasing the ATP payroll tax from present levels to perhaps 17.5 percent at the end of this decade and to 34.0 percent by the year 2020 would, in turn, drastically reduce the real disposable income of the working population and thus cause further harm to the economy.

There are several ways to cope with this problem. One is to reduce pension claims; another would broaden the tax base; still a third would change other social benefits designed for

Table 4

Payroll Tax Necessary for a Pay-as-You-Go System
(percentage of taxable income)

Year	Annual real wage increase	
	None	3%
1980	9.5	9.5
1985	13.6	10.7
1990	17.5	12.5
1995	20.0	13.8
2000	22.1	15.0
2005	24.6	16.8
2010	28.4	19.7
2015	32.4	22.7
2020	34.4	24.2

groups older than 65 years. There are indications that all three ways will be tried. To avoid excessive taxation of the working population, the recent manipulation of the index, the abolition of the floor and ceiling for taxable incomes, and the automatic reduction of housing benefits when pensions rise all involve changes in other measures to compensate for increases in ATP transfers.

EFFECTS ON SAVINGS AND THE CAPITAL MARKET

The effect of this system on individuals' incentives could be disastrous. If an individual really believed that the next generation would show him the same generosity as he has shown to his parents' generation, he would have little motivation for long-term saving over the life cycle.

The evidence supports this conclusion, as the financial net savings are close to zero or even negative for the household sector as a whole (see table 5). Negative rates of interest (after inflation and taxation) give small incentives for saving in nominal assets. The equity market is small, and the total value of wealth in equities held by households is about 30 billion SEK—little more than one year's basic pensions. Real savings, however—invested, for the most part, in owner-occupied houses—are positive, owing to the favorable tax treatment of homeowners compared with that of tenants.

Table 5

Household Savings
(billion SEK)

Year	Net financial savings
1971	0.8
1972	—2.6
1973	—1.7
1974	0.1
1975	0.0
1976	—4.2
1977	—2.2
1978	—0.5
1979	—2.1

The main effect of the dominance of pay-as-you-go and comprehensive social welfare systems is that no large group in Swedish society depends directly on high returns from financial assets. At the same time, everyone—the government, tenants, home-owners, farmers, and even industrialists—wants to see low interest rates. Regulation of interest rates and strong government interference in the capital market thus have met little political resistance. Well-organized pressure groups support the policy, and pensioners—present or future—do not suffer directly.

However, the policy does damage some of the mechanisms of the market economy. Although forced saving, as in the ATP, can partly compensate for disincentives to individual saving, no natural incentives exist for the ATP fund to maximize the yield on its investments. Legal restrictions on investment—which favor government and mortgage institutions—affect not only the ATP fund but also the SPP, private insurance companies, and banks.

Looking another way at the effect on saving, the present fund, with a value of 150 billion SEK, would be sufficient—depending on real rates of interest—to pay the next eight to ten years' of ATP claims for those who have now reached the age of 65. This means that ATP claims are now very large compared with the fund. Calculations are, of course, uncertain because individual claims depend on future individual incomes. But it seems reasonable to assume that, if the ATP had been completely funded, its present value would be between 500 and 1,000 billion SEK.

Similar calculations can be done, of course, for the other pay-as-you-go components of the redistribution. This makes it clear that a system based on funded transfers would have drastically changed the working of the whole economy and resulted in a classical Keynesian problem of oversaving.

There is thus a general problem of finding the right mix between funding and paying as you go. The present Swedish system seems to offer a somewhat extreme solution, with its almost complete reliance on pay-as-you-go and its corresponding negative effects on individual saving, and with a need for enforced saving through government to maintain the overall saving ratio in the economy.

POSSIBLE EFFECTS ON EMPLOYMENT

The transfer system to the elderly might affect employment, mainly for those groups around the pension age. In table 6 the development of the labor market participation rate is indicated for the groups 55-64 and 65-74 years of age. It is obvious that participation rates substantially decline for the groups above 65 (the pension age was 67 until 1976, when it was lowered to 65 years). A corresponding decrease around the falling trend for male participation can be found for the same year. But even more interesting is the long-term decline in participation rates for men, both below and above the official pension age.

Table 6

Labor Market Participation Rate

Year	Men		Women	
	55-64	65-74	55-64	65-74
1965	88.3	37.7	39.2	11.6
1970	85.8	28.2	44.1	9.1
1975	82.0	19.9	49.6	6.1
1980	78.7	14.2	55.3	3.7

The disincentives for labor market participation operate mainly in two ways. First, there is an income effect which allows a pensioner with increasing pensions and benefits in kind not only to survive, but to live a rather comfortable life without working. Second, high marginal tax rates on earned income, combined with the means test for pensions, may substantially decrease disposable wage income from work. As already mentioned, the special additions to the basic pension and housing benefits are decreased automatically if the person receives income other than the basic pension. Combining a marginal tax rate of about 30 percent in the lowest income brackets (above the basic pension) with a reduction of housing benefits of 33 percent, a person with the basic pension is likely to face an effective total marginal tax rate of 63 percent. It is reasonable to assume that such high tax rates at low-income levels will drastically reduce work incentives.

The increase in female labor-market participation in the age group 55-64 can also be partially explained by the social security system. Women entering the labor market late are heavily overcompensated, as an extra year of work still substantially increase the pension claims on the ATP pension system.

REDISTRIBUTION BETWEEN GENERATIONS

Table 7 summarizes the different systems. Some of the estimates are speculative, but the total sum of the redistribution still indicates many of the problems faced by a country with an aging stable population and a strong egalitarian political tradition.

Basic pensions are indexed to inflation, though the index does not fully compensate for all changes in the consumer price index. Housing benefits are related to actual rents and housing costs. The supplementary pension scheme (ATP) provides indexed pensions related to previous income. This part of the total redistribution system is now growing as each new generation entering the system registers the full qualification time. This increase will automatically reduce housing benefits and the means-tested supplements to the basic pension. As discussed earlier, the role of the fund will decrease as current tax income comes into balance with pension payments.

Health care and social services are included in this chapter because they are important transfers which can be translated into cash terms. If health care had been financed by age-related insurance premiums instead of by a proportional income tax, one would expect the annual premium to be about 2,000 SEK for individuals aged 35 to 44, but around 10,000 to 15,000 SEK for individuals over 70. At present, the basic pension benefit is 15,300 SEK per year. A market approach to health care would thus imply that the pension level should be increased considerably, and should be almost doubled for the very old. One way of looking at the transfers taking place in the Swedish health care system is to note that the main redistribution of income

Table 7

Total Income and Consumption of Age Groups above 65 Years of Age, 1979 (billion SEK)

System	Gross[a]	Net[b]	Indexed	Pay-as-you-go
Basic pensions	28.5	24.0	Yes	Yes
Housing benefits	4.0	4.0	No	Yes[c]
Supplementary pension (ATP)	15.8	13.0	Yes	Yes
Health care	20.5	20.5	—	Yes[c]
Local government services	8.0	8.0	—	Yes[c]
Negotiated pensions:				
Government	3.0	2.5	Yes	Yes
Private	5.0	4.0	No	Partly funded
Taxes and out-of-pocket costs for social services	NA[d]	10.0	—	—
Financial and real dissaving	NA[d]	NA[d]	—	—
Total		66.0		
Memorandum items:				
GDP at market prices	456.0			
Total individual consumption[e]	340.0			

[a]Including survivors and those who retired early.

[b]Excluding those under 65 years of age.

[c]Tax-financed and generally not regarded as part of social security.

[d]NA = not available.

[e]Including all private and public consumption except for collective items such as defense, crime prevention, and basic research; also included are individual items such as education, day-care centers, health care, etc.

and consumption takes place between generations, and not between the healthy and the sick or the rich and the poor.

Health care and "free" social services together constitute a program as large as the basic pension scheme. Most social services provided by the government are age-related: education and day-care centers, for instance, do not help the retired.

Mature people working full time are generally low consumers of public social services (although they benefit from other public programs, such as salaries).

While Sweden's few funded private pension plans involve no redistribution, some private schemes show strong similarities to pay-as-you-go social security systems, thus involving important redistributional elements.

To construct a complete income report for the elderly requires information about what they pay in taxes and in out-of-pocket costs for health care and the other social services. Data, however, are scarce. In a rough calculation, if it is assumed that supplementary pensions and negotiated pensions are taxed at an average rate of 45 percent and that out-of-pocket costs amount to 10 percent of the social services' bill, the amount could be about 10 billion SEK.

The last item is dissaving, both financial and real (except for pension insurance). We have no data whatsoever for this item and I hesitate to guess. There are indications that some groups of retired persons can save; a possible case would be a person in a long-term medical ward (paying perhaps 30 SEK per day on an actual cost of 500 to 600 SEK per day) with a full basic pension and a supplementary pension or some kind of negotiated pension. Having limited consumption opportunities, he is likely to save or to transfer funds back to the younger generation. A good guess, however, is that financial dissaving plays no significant role in determining the consumption standard of retired people. In 1975 only 12 percent of all households had a total wealth above 200,000 SEK, an amount roughly equal to the actuarial value of the basic pension at the age of 65. Most individual wealth consists of owner-occupied houses, summer houses, and small farms. According to a life-cycle hypothesis, one would expect a real dissaving or increasing mortgages in later years of life in order to spread consumption over the years. With our present knowledge, it is very difficult to estimate the possible size of real disinvestments.

Some uncertainty remains. Disregarding possible dissaving, taxes, and out-of-pocket costs, we will end with the rather bewildering conclusion that the 16 percent of all Swedes over 65 years of age consume 22 percent of total individual consumption—i.e., private and public consumption—less collective services such as defense, crime prevention, and basic research. Thus current redistribution gives the elderly a consumption standard far above the average Swede's. Assuming that taxes and out-of-pocket costs for social services amount to 10 billion SEK, the consumption potential would be a more realistic 19 percent—still giving a more than proportional share to the elderly. This share can, of course, be increased by dissaving.

It should be observed that, out of the 76 billion SEK transferred to the elderly, only 4 billion SEK pass through funded systems; the rest is conveyed through pay-as-you-go systems financed out of general taxes.

REDISTRIBUTION WITHIN GENERATIONS

In limiting the discussion to the supplementary pension system (ATP), the present rules (a thirty-year qualification period and averaging the fifteen best income years) will have some rather obvious effects. To begin with, professionals with many years of education will generally have no problem in qualifying, but will pay premiums for a shorter period than male blue-collar workers. Blue-collar workers with very long qualification periods will be at a disadvantage compared, for example, with housewives who have had a small wage income for many years and full-time work late in life. To understand why, let us take two somewhat extreme cases—the first, a blue-collar worker earning a rather constant income between the ages of 16 and 65 (we assume he will never have an income above half of the pension system's ceiling), and the second, a housewife who does not start full-time work until the age of 50, but has had sporadic work with a wage income adequate to provide fifteen registered qualification years. At 50, she acquires an academic degree—which is heavily subsidized—and holds a professional job for fifteen years with an income at the ceiling. Her ATP pension will be twice the size of the blue-collar worker's pension, although her premiums are about half the size of his.

This example is deliberately extreme, but it is obvious that income redistributions of this sort are intentional. The whole ATP system was constructed at a time when male full-time workers constituted the main part of the labor force, and it has not yet been adapted to the increased participation of part-time female workers. It is even possible to explain the increasing number of females working part time—partially, at least—by the high benefits they can anticipate from the pension system (and from other social security systems, such as unemployment benefits) in return for low tax contributions.

SOME POLITICAL NOTES

In the 1957 referendum, the principal alternatives were a funded system and a negotiated system of the SPP type versus a pay-as-you-go system, such as the ATP, with some enforced saving. The ATP system's victory, considering its political backing, can be explained simply. The generation close to retirement age at the introduction of a pay-as-you-go system will gain compared with a funded system, an effect reinforced by the lower qualification period for the older age groups. Those who will pay a large part of the pension claims of the present working generation were too young at that time to have voted for the system.

There is a strong tendency for political decisions to benefit well-organized and easily identifiable groups while diffusing the costs over large, unorganized groups. In the case of social security, the costs were to be borne by nonvoting generations; thus the rejection of the funded system and the market approach was no surprise.

This tendency was obvious during the 1970s. In 1976 the pension age was decreased from 67 to 65 years, and some favorable rules were introduced for retirement at half pension at the age of 62. The beneficiaries of this reform are easy to identify, and political parties addressed their appeals directly to them. They said very little about the costs. The immediate effect was a small rise in the premium level and a decrease in enforced saving in the ATP fund.

One possible conclusion is that proposals for pay-as-you-go systems give a political advantage to the groups above and close to retirement age. Their apparently disproportionate share of consumption resources may be interpreted as indicating their strong political power.

NOTES ON THE FUTURE

Disregarding for the moment the small number of funded group plans such as the SPP, the entire Swedish social security system is based on the pay-as-you-go principle and is government financed and administered. This means that, other than the ATP component, there is no relationship between taxes paid and individual benefits received, although some taxes have misleading labels such as the "basic pension payroll tax". Even for the income-related ATP, there is no simple relationship between an individual's contributions and his future benefits, partly because of the complicated rules for calculating qualification periods and benefits. During recent years there has been an increasing tendency to dissolve the clear relationship between contributions paid and benefits received in the ATP system—e.g., with the proposal to abolish the income ceiling for contributions but to keep it for benefits.

Given these financing principles, it is obvious that marginal tax rates—including income taxes and payroll taxes—will be high for the working population. Public spending at present runs at about 65 percent of Sweden's GDP, and recent budget deficits amount to almost 5 percent of GDP. To support this level of spending, marginal tax rates have been raised to levels where they stifle industrial productivity. Much of this spending seems to maintain the consumption level of the over-65s, which gives this age group an excessive share of the material product.

The problem in relation to the elderly is aggravated by the general aging of the Swedish population. Since 1960 the proportion of the elderly (over 65) has increased from 12 percent to 16 percent of the population, and of the over-75s—who make significantly higher demands on the health and social welfare services—has increased from 4 percent to 6 percent.

Reversing the trend toward ever-increasing expenditures may be accomplished in many different ways, and a multitude of plans has been discussed. Higher out-of-pocket costs for health care and social services have been investigated, but are meeting substantial political resistance. For most of the services given in kind to the elderly, it is proposed that strict budget limits be imposed by the central government on the responsible county and local governments. But this raises crucial constitutional questions concerning the latter's independent status.

One interesting possibility lies in reforming the ATP by emphasizing the program as an insurance system of earned entitlements, thus reversing the tendency to obscure the relation between contributions and benefits. A stricter relationship between contributions paid and pensions received would drastically cut marginal tax rates, since contributions would be regarded as insurance-premium contributions and not as taxes. This would mean, for instance, that pensions would be calculated as direct averages of all previous income, rather than of income from the best fifteen years out of thirty. An additional possibility would gradually transform at least parts of the ATP system into a funded scheme with pensions dependent on the financial yield of the fund's investments. This would strengthen efficiency incentives in the capital market and decrease the role of forced savings in government funds.

It is obvious that many of the various social services, those which require little or no out-of-pocket costs, might become unnecessary as the ATP scheme gradually extends to a larger proportion of the population and gives a majority of the elderly the opportunity to pay for the services they use. This would entail an increased reliance on a means test.

There are a number of ways to solve the many problems now afflicting the Swedish social security system. In considering their options, policymakers face a circular dilemma: the future performance of the social security system depends on the future performance of the Swedish economy, which in turn will be strongly influenced by the means chosen to solve the social security problems. Much is at stake, and it can be hoped that policymakers will take a longer view of these problems than they have in the past.

7

MARTIN C. JANSSEN
HEINZ H. MÜLLER

Switzerland

The three-component system: federal insurance, supplementary pension fund, individual provision. Tax and revenue provisions. Short- and long-run financial performance. Effect on savings, investment, employment. Distributional aspects. Future developments. Suggested reforms.

The Swiss social security system has three parts—a basic program, which provides minimum protection; a supplementary program, now voluntary but undergoing changes which will make it mandatory; and invididual provision.

The basic program is a state-run, pay-as-you-go system which, according to the federal constitution, is supposed to "cover basic needs." The program is financed about 80.0 percent by a payroll tax of 8.4 percent, shared equally by employer and employee, with no ceiling on earnings on which the tax is levied. Of the balance, some 16.0 percent comes from a transfer of general revenues and the rest from returns on a trust fund. Contributions from all these sources amounted to 5.8 percent of gross national product (GNP) in 1978.[1]

In 1980 basic program benefits were payable to men at age 65 and to women at 62 in amounts varying between 6,600 Swiss francs (Sfr., $3,227 U.S. at an exchange rate of $0.489 as of 1 July 1981), and 13,200 Sfr. ($6,455) per year, depending on contributions. Couples receive half as much again. All benefits are indexed to compensate for price inflation, but for only 50 percent of real wage increases. Widows and orphans also receive benefits, and there are supplementary payments for elderly people with low incomes.

The supplementary program is currently (1981) a voluntary funded plan organized by private and public employers, with contributions—amounting to 4.1 percent of GNP in 1978—to 17,000 participating private and public pension funds. There were 1.6 million contributors in 1978, and 320,000 beneficiaries. At present, payroll taxes for the supplementary programs come to about 6.4 percent, paid two-thirds by employers on average. Although the precise shape of the new mandatory program is uncertain as of this writing, payroll taxes for the new supplementary program, unless there is another referendum, may rise to 15.0 percent. The new pensions will combine with the basic pension to equal 60.0 percent of last earnings for about 40.0 percent of today's regular employees. At the other end of the spectrum, about one in five of these employees is covered only by the basic program.

The third component—individual provision—includes all forms of private saving, including private life insurance. In 1978 this diverse package amounted to 2.9 percent of GNP, of which private insurance accounted for 1.4 percent.

In 1980 there were 3.6 workers paying into the system for each retiree receiving benefits—which is better than the situation in most other countries in this book. However, as in other countries, the Swiss population is aging, and the ratio of workers to retirees is expected to fall to 2.2 in 2020 and to 1.8 in 2030. These future changes will bring significant stresses on the social security system; their severity will depend on future economic growth, among other factors. With 2.0 percent real growth, the basic program payroll tax thus will have to rise from 8.4 percent to 10.6 percent in the year 2030; but with no real growth, it will have to rise to 17.1 percent to maintain currently legislated benefits.

Since the supplementary program is funded, it is not vulnerable to demographic changes as is the pay-as-you-go basic system. Nevertheless, in light of the reforms now being developed, its future will depend very much on how it is structured. Both alternatives now being debated would introduce pay-as-you-go elements. The new supplementary program, which will be structured to maintain contributions of 15 percent of payroll, will provide some (not full) indexation for inflation. This formula will limit stresses on the supplementary program by allowing benefits to decline as a percentage of last earnings.

The effect of the new supplementary program on saving could be harmful. There is already evidence that steady expansion of the two public programs has reduced individual provision for retirement a great deal over the last ten years. In terms of disposable income, for instance, the private saving rate fell by about 50 percent between 1970 and 1978, and it is likely that any extension of benefits on a pay-as-you-go basis would reduce it further. In contrast, a fully funded program would increase saving and investment, and therefore future economic growth.

As in France, Switzerland has no earnings test, so the system does not directly discourage employment. However, earnings over 9,000 Sfr ($4,401) *are* subject to the normal payroll tax, without enhancing future benefits. At the same time, the introduction of certain pay-as-you-go elements in the new supplementary program will create serious disincentives to hire people over 55 years of age.

Like most systems, the Swiss redistributes wealth from the young to the old and from men to women. There is also a redistribution to the self-employed—who pay the tax at a lower rate of 7.8 percent—and, because of the benefit formula, to people with higher than normal income increases during their careers.

Although the Swiss system is free of many of the difficulties which plague other countries, specific problems remain—involving both financing and equity—which the government will have to face, particularly in deciding how to extend the supplementary program.

BACKGROUND

In 1925 Swiss voters accepted a constitutional amendment which allowed for a basic program of state-run old-age and survivors insurance financed by a payroll tax and state contributions. The necessary legislation finally passed in 1947, more than twenty years later. This program is the basic part of the Swiss social security system and is compulsory for everyone. It is based on a pay-as-you-go system and has been extended several times. Today (1981) the payroll tax is 8.4 percent, shared by employers and employees, and benefits for single persons vary between 6,600 Sfr.[2] and 13,200 Sfr. per year according to contributions. Benefits for couples are 50 percent higher.[3]

The supplementary program dates back to the nineteenth century when private pension funds came into existence—partly to reinforce ties between skilled employees and firms, partly in response to fiscal legislation. Although this supplementary program is not yet compulsory, it included over 17,000 pension funds in 1978 with total reserves of more than 74 billion Sfr. (47.3 percent of GNP).

OUTLOOK

The future of the three-component system will be determined by the 1972 amendment to the federal constitution:

The Confederation shall adopt measures necessary to promote an adequate insurance scheme for old-age, death, and disability. This scheme shall be provided for by a *federal insurance* [scheme; basic component], by a *pension fund scheme* [supplementary component] and by *individual provision* [individual component]. [Italics added]

The basic component essentially conforms to this constitutional amendment. The tenth revision at present is under discussion, a revision which would improve the position of women and would allow for flexible retirement.

As for the supplementary program, each of the two legislative houses has produced a bill on how to implement the 1972 amendment. Both bills are based on the present scheme. They would introduce pay-as-you-go elements and compulsory membership, and would guarantee mobility between pension funds. The House of Representatives wants to provide benefits which, combined with the basic component, would equal 60 percent of an individual's last pay. A large pay-as-you-go element would be necessary to accomplish this. By comparison, the Senate prefers to emphasize contributions, allowing a smaller pay-as-you-go element and probably leading to lower benefits.

SHORT- AND LONG-RUN FINANCIAL PERFORMANCE OF THE THREE-COMPONENT SYSTEM

The basic program

As already mentioned, the basic program is compulsory for everyone. Old-age benefits are paid from the age of 65 for men and 62 for women. In March 1979, 534,000 single persons and 228,000 married couples were receiving benefits. Widows (not widowers) and orphans also receive benefits, and there are supplementary payments for low-income people older than 65 (62). These benefits are financed principally by a payroll tax equal to 8.4 percent of wage income with no upper limit, half of this tax formally paid by the employer (the rate is slightly lower for self-employed people). In addition, there is a government contribution out of general revenues (16.0 percent of total outlays in 1979) and interest from a modest trust fund (3.3 percent of total outlays in 1979), the fund itself valued at about one-year's outlay. Since employers formally pay half the payroll tax, political pressures led to a tax reduction for self-employed people—even though most economists agree that the employer's contribution is really paid by employees in the form of reduced wages.

Payroll tax rates, general revenue contributions, and benefits have changed several times since 1948, as shown in tables 1 and 2 and in figure 1. Table 2 shows the average relative shares of payroll tax, direct government contributions, and interest

Table 1

Payroll Tax Rates: The Basic Program

Total Payroll Tax	Employees	Self-employed
1948-1968	4.0%	4.0%
1969-1972	5.2	4.6
1973-1975[a]	7.8	6.8
1975[b]-1978	8.4	7.3
Since 1979	8.4	7.8

Source: Müller 1978, p. 132.

[a]30 June 1975.

[b]1 July 1975.

Table 2

Revenue Sources: The Basic Program

Period	Payroll tax	Direct government contributions	Interest from trust fund
1948-1957	71.1%	21.6%	7.3%
1958-1967	71.7	15.2	13.1
1968-1976	76.6	16.4	7.0

Source: Müller 1978, p. 136.

from the trust fund. Principal changes in the development of nominal benefits are shown in figure 1. (During this period the consumer price index rose from 100.0 in 1948 to 233.0 in 1977, while the index of individual wages rose from 100.0 to 557.4.)

During the start-up phase, the first generation of beneficiaries was treated favorably and a trust fund was accumulated. The government believed, however, that the trust fund was growing unnecessarily fast in relation to outlays.[4] In subsequent years, therefore, benefits were increased without further increases in payroll taxes. Combined with unfavorable demographic trends, the result was that between 1956 and 1978

Figure 1
Benefits for Single Persons since 1948

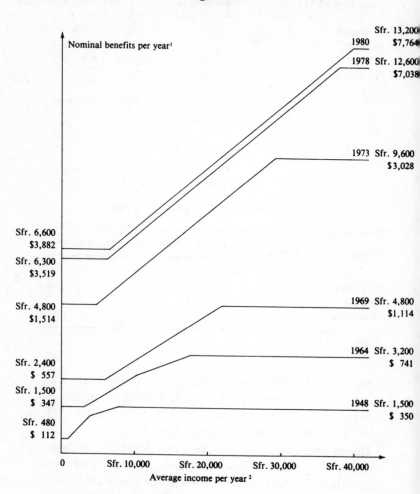

¹Not adjusted for inflation.
²On which benefits are calculated.

the trust fund declined from eight yearly outlays to one. The payroll tax and benefits increased during the 1960s and early 1970s (see table 1 and figure 1). Given a reluctance to further increase the payroll tax, a "combined index" was introduced which compensates fully for price inflation but for only 50 percent of real wage increases.

A critical part of projected tax rates involves demographic projections. Like all industrial countries, Switzerland faces an aging of its population which will strain the system's ability to pay currently legislated benefits. The most significant factor here concerns the decline in number of workers in relation to retirees; as shown by table 3, at present there are 3.6 workers paying for each retiree, but that number will decline to 2.2 by the year 2020 and to 1.8 in 2030.

Table 3

Ratio of Workers to Retirees

Year	Ratio
1980	3.6
1985	3.6
1990	3.6
1995	3.4
2000	3.2
2010	2.8
2020	2.2

Making assumptions about the future growth rate of real wages and demographic developments and assuming state contributions of 20 percent, table 4 shows the future payroll tax rates necessary to support benefits at currently legislated levels. Because of uncertainty in demographic forecasts, the figures in table 4—especially those for the years 2010 and 2020—are not very reliable.

Table 4

Projected Payroll Tax Rates:[a] The Basic Program

Year	Growth rate of real wages =	
	0%	2%
1980	8.4%	8.4%
1985	8.6	8.2
1990	9.1	8.3
1995	9.6	8.4
2000	11.4	9.5
2010	12.3	9.3
2020	14.7	10.0

Source: Authors' computations based on official data.

[a]The total payroll tax is split evenly between employer and employee.

Given a 2.0 percent annual growth in real wages, a real interest rate of 0.5 percent, and certain other assumptions, table 5 shows total payroll contributions as a percentage of total benefits for three age levels. It also shows the internal rate of return.[5] It can be seen from table 5 that the present value of benefits exceeds the present value of contributions for everyone. Furthermore, comparing these figures with those in table 8 below, one can see that the basic component was a good "investment," especially for elderly and low-income people. Hence a person of 63 drawing maximum benefits invested a relatively large amount at a real interest rate of 7.0 percent, while a person of the same age drawing minimum benefits invested a relatively small amount at 11.6 percent. Considering a real interest rate on government bonds of about 1.0 percent, the transfers to both groups are substantial. But despite the higher return for lower-income retirees, many higher-income retirees enjoy much higher actual money transfers. Therefore, the widespread opinion that low-income people benefit more under the basic program than those with higher incomes is clearly mistaken.

Table 5

Redistribution and Rates of Return:
The Basic Program

Age of individual in 1978	Minimum benefits from annual income of Sfr. 6,300		Maximum benefits from annual income of Sfr. 37,800	
	Contributions as % of benefits (present values)	Internal rate of return[a]	Ratio between present values	Internal rate of return[a]
20	32.1%	4.1%	96.3%	0.7%
40	22.8	5.6	68.5	1.8
63	7.6	11.6	22.7	7.0

Source: Hauser and Meyer 1980, Tables 2 and 6.

[a]Hypothetical interest rate leading to equality of the present values of total payroll contributions and total benefits.

The supplementary program

Since Parliament has not yet passed a bill implementing the 1972 constitutional amendment, the supplementary program is still nonmandatory. In 1978 it consisted of 17,000 pension funds (organized by private and public employers) with 1.6 million contributing members and 320,000 beneficiaries.

Employers paid about two-thirds of the contributions in 1978, with employees paying the balance. The trust funds of the supplementary program increased from 8.4 billion Sfr. (28.2 percent of GNP) in 1956 to 74.3 billion Sfr. (47.3 percent of GNP) in 1978, yielding a capital income of 3.2 billion Sfr. in that year. While contributions and benefits remained almost constant in terms of GNP, the trust funds grew rapidly.

More than 50 percent of the trust funds are invested in bonds and in direct credits to private and public employers, almost 20 percent in real estate, 10 percent in mortgages, and between 5 percent and 10 percent in stocks. Today about 40 percent of all regular employees will receive, from a combination of the basic and supplementary programs, pensions equal to at least 60 percent of their last pay. At the other end of the scale, about 20 percent of these employees are covered only by the basic program.

Table 6

Contributions and Benefits: The Supplementary Program

Period	Average contributions per year (in billion Sfr.)	Average benefits per year (in billion Sfr.)
1955-1959	1.2 (3.9% of GNP)	0.6 (1.9% of GNP)
1960-1964	1.9 (4.1% of GNP)	0.9 (2.0% of GNP)
1965-1969	2.8 (4.0% of GNP)	1.3 (1.8% of GNP)
1970-1974	4.5 (3.7% of GNP)	1.7 (1.4% of GNP)
1975-1978	6.4 (4.3% of GNP)	2.8 (1.8% of GNP)

Source: Switzerland, *Die Volkswirtschaft.*

The third component: individual provision

The individual component includes such private provision as life insurance, securities, bank deposits, and real estate.[6] Although the figures (see note 6) suggest that individual provision is quite important, it is noteworthy that the saving rate of private households fell from 11.5 percent of disposable income in 1971 to 4.6 percent in 1978.

Table 7 illustrates the development of the three-component system in terms of contributions. The extension of the basic program has been accompanied by a decline in the rate of private saving. The substitution between the three programs is discussed in detail below.

Table 7

Contribution Rates:
The Three Components

Year	Payroll tax (basic program) as % of wage income	Contributions (supplementary program) as % of employees' total wages	Saving rate as % of disposable income	Index of real GNP
1968	4.0	7.2	7.3	100.0
1970	5.2	7.1	8.9	109.3
1972	5.2	7.1	10.0	114.9
1974	7.8	7.0	9.7	119.6
1976	8.4	7.4	5.5	111.6
1978	8.4	7.5	4.6	115.1

Source: Switzerland, *Die Volkswirtschaft*; idem, *Statistisches Jahrbuch der Schweiz.*

Basic program versus pension funds as investment opportunities

Comparing the basic and the supplementary programs is difficult, since the latter is essentially a pay-as-you-go scheme while the former is funded. Under pay-as-you-go, working generations pay social security taxes to support retired generations, and in turn are supported in their retirement by the working generation that follows them. Assuming that the population growth rate, technological progress, and life expectancy all remain constant, pay-as-you-go schemes have an internal rate of return equal to the sum of the growth rates of the population and of real wages. It is important to understand that the internal rate does not depend on life expectancy. (For a detailed explanation, cf. Rosen 1977, pp. 91-93.) Thus to some extent, if we exclude some economic side effects, the growth rate of total real wage income is an approximation of the internal rate of return in a pay-as-you-go scheme after the start-up phase.[7]

Table 8 enables us to compare the three components as investment opportunities. For the reasons mentioned, column (5) of this table approximates the performance of an imaginary pay-as-you-go scheme; column (2) refers to the supplementary program, and columns (3) and (4) to the private program.

Table 8

Investment Opportunities: The Three Components

Period	Real rate of return:			Growth rate: total real wage income
	Pension funds	Government bonds	Stocks	
(1)	(2)	(3)	(4)	(5)
1949-1958	—	2.1%	—	3.9%
1959-1968	—	0.3	11.5%	6.3
1969-1978	— 0.3%	0.2	— 2.9	3.3
1959-1978	—	0.3	4.1	4.8
1949-1978	—	0.9	—	4.5

Sources: Switzerland, *Die Volkswirtschaft*; idem, *AHV-Lohnstatistik*; Swiss Bank Corporation, *Index of the Stock Market*; authors' computations.

From table 8, it is tempting to say that—in terms of their respective internal rates and excluding benefits to initial generations—pay-as-you-go financing yields better long-term results than full funding. However, a few points must be considered. First, transitory effects may make the growth rate of total real wage income a bad approximation for the actual long-run internal rate of return of a pay-as-you-go system. Second, the rate of return on pension funds is probably underestimated, because capital gains are typically excluded from official statistics. Third, much of the pensions' trust funds is invested in bonds or is loaned as credits used to finance real capital. Since a gap exists between the marginal productivity of capital and the real interest rate on bonds (this gap is partly due to the investment policies of financial institutions which are influenced by government regulations), the *social return* on pension funds is higher than the direct rate given in table 8.

Accumulated savings generated by fully funded pension funds yield special income effects. First, inducing increases in the capital stock tends to raise the marginal productivity of labor (cf. Rosen 1977, p. 94), which in turn—given current economic conditions—leads to higher wages. Second, the financial institutions' investment policies tend to reduce the rate of return to the typical owner of domestic bonds. Third, two opposite effects may result from a higher stock of real capital for a typical holder of Swiss shares: while the marginal productivity of capital declines, firms tend to issue more bonds or to take more credits directly from their pension funds and thus take advantage of the difference between the marginal productivity of capital and the real interest rate on bonds.

Beyond these long-run aspects, what are the short-run implications of a marginal change in the financing system? To move from full funding toward pay-as-you-go is easy, since it leads to short-run "benefits" during the start-up phase; a move in the opposite direction is more difficult, as it entails short-run "costs." In the last section, we will argue that the Swiss system has evolved into a sound combination of full funding and pay-as-you-go financing, in contrast with most of the countries described in other chapters.

INFLUENCE OF THE THREE PROGRAMS ON SAVING AND INVESTMENT

Effects on saving

For an individual, the three parts of the Swiss social security system represent alternative ways to save. It is reasonable, therefore, to expect changes in the size of the first and second programs to influence the third, which is private saving.

Interpreting household data for 1971-1975, the following conclusions can be drawn (Oberhänsli 1981, part 5):

1. In terms of contributions, the rate of substitution between the basic program and private saving seems to be almost one to one.[8] This means that a dollar added to payroll taxes means a dollar off private saving. Between 1971 and 1975, however, payroll taxes were raised from 5.2 percent to 8.4 percent—in effect, creating a new start-up phase. During a start-up phase the expected additional benefits considerably exceed the additional contributions. Therefore, in terms of benefits, the rate of substitution between the basic program and private saving would be much lower than one to one.

2. In terms of contributions, the rate of substitution between the basic and the supplementary programs is positive but lower than that between the first and third programs. This result is not surprising, since the present value of benefits cannot exceed the present value of contributions in a funded scheme. Benefits might well be below contributions, in fact, since employees lose a substantial part of their benefits if they change from one firm to another.

Recent evidence shows the surprising conclusion that the saving rate of retirees in Switzerland is some 60 percent higher than that of workers (Schweizer 1980, p. 124).

In judging overall impacts from data presented by Oberhänsli (1981) and Schweizer (1980), we can conclude that in the near future (a) extending retirement benefits on the basis of a pay-as-you-go system would reduce overall saving, and (b) extending benefits on the basis of full funding would raise saving at least slightly. In the long run, full funding would result in higher saving than would pay-as-you-go.

Effects on investment

Additional savings do not necessarily mean additional real capital. Empirical evidence suggests the following conclusions:

first, partial replacement of individual provision by the basic pay-as-you-go component would reduce capital formation. Second, since federal, state, and local government deficits and borrowing amounted only to 31.5 percent of the total increase in pension reserves during the last ten years, we may assume that a fair part of the funded supplementary program must have been used to finance the formation of real capital. And third, considering the particular rates of substitution between the different components, it follows that the partial replacement of pay-as-you-go financing by full funding would increase the capital stock. International capital flows are not expected to invalidate these conclusions.

EFFECTS ON EMPLOYMENT

In Switzerland there is no earnings test, which means that people over 65 years of age (women, over 62) are entitled to benefits whether they are employed or not. However, wage income above 9,000 Sfr. ($5,300) is subject to the normal payroll tax and future benefits do not depend on these contributions.

According to a recent study (Schweizer 1980, pp. 64-65, 247-48), 31.7 percent of all persons over 65 (62) were employed in 1970. This compares with about 25.0 percent in the United States and some 16.0 percent in West Germany (Belbin 1978, pp. 135-37). The figure is probably much lower today, partly because of a slump in the economy in 1974-1975, and partly because of employers' changes in retirement policies.

Employed people over 65 (62) have higher incomes, more wealth, and a higher saving rate than retired people over 65 (62 [Schweizer 1980, p. 65]). It thus seems that a further extension of collective provision for old-age would not substantially influence employment of the elderly.

REDISTRIBUTIONAL EFFECTS

The basic program

The main redistributional effects of the current system result from the basic program. Characteristic features of a tax-financed transfer system are as follows:

- Favorable treatment is given to initial generations.
- Government contributions are financed directly out of general revenues.[9]
- There are upper and lower bounds on benefits, but no bounds on contributions.
- Women receive privileged treatment in some aspects.
- Singles are treated differently from couples.
- There are differential tax rates for self-employed people.
- Contributions of employees over 65 (62) do not influence their benefits.

Intergenerational transfer: treatment of initial generations

The start and subsequent extension of the basic social security programs have created several initial generations. Table 5 shows that the expected present value of payroll tax contributions is less than 25 percent of the corresponding present value of benefits for people born before 1915. Moreover, the ratio between contributions and benefits favors low-income people. As mentioned, however, for some high-income people the expected value of benefits exceeds the corresponding value of contributions by a larger amount than that for low-income people—a condition which has been criticized for a long time.[10]

Intragenerational transfers

Beyond the transfer from young people to old, other redistributions occur under the basic program:

- From men to women, because women get retirement benefits from the age of 62 (men from 65) and have a greater life expectancy.

• From employees to self-employed people, because the latter pay less than the total payroll tax paid by an employee and his employer. This conclusion rests on the widely accepted assumption that an employee in fact bears the total payroll tax (cf., e.g., Friedman 1977, pp. 25-27), even the portion ostensibly borne by the employer. This conclusion has been questioned in political debates, the argument being made that in some cases employees bear less than 100 percent of the tax. Political considerations account for the difference in the payroll tax for employees and self-employed people.

• Analysis of the transfer between singles and couples is complex.[11] In the case of married couples with low incomes, there is an incentive to divorce and to draw benefits individually. In the case of married couples with incomes above a certain level, divorce would pay if both partners contributed more than a minimum amount to their combined income. In the range between, the result depends on individual circumstances.

• There is a transfer in favor of people with higher than normal income increases during their careers. This is because benefits are not based on the current value of contributions but on the mean of nominal wage income during the period of contributions, multiplied by a factor adjusting in particular for inflation. This means, for instance, that—for any one individual—a dollar contributed in 1948 has the same influence on benefits as a dollar contributed in 1968.

Transfers among different regions of the country

The basic component also redistributes from urban to rural areas—in 1976 some 500 million Sfr. ($200 million). This results from the lower per capital income and the larger number of retired people living in rural areas.

SUMMARY, OUTLOOK, AND OBSERVATIONS

Four major issues remain: How appropriate is the three-component retirement system to the past and future situation of Switzerland? What are the effects of its present implementation? What is the institutional and economic context of the planned extension of the second component? And what problems, if any, will result from that planned extension?

Rationale for the current system

Several reasons are cited to justify mandatory collective provision[12] for old-age. An individual does not know how long he will live, and life insurance is the only form of private provision protecting against this uncertainty. But adverse selection makes private life insurance relatively expensive (cf. Feldstein 1977, pp. 17-19). Moreover, if there were no mandatory insurance, and extensive means-tested welfare program would be necessary for political reasons. At the same time, there would continue to be deserving poor people who would be reluctant to claim benefits under such a program. The politically optimal level of mandatory insurance ultimately depends on balancing the reduction in individual freedom which it entails against the relative advantages of collective insurance.

To determine how the financing of mandatory insurance should be apportioned between full funding and pay-as-you-go, it is necessary to compare the investment opportunities of the two financing systems in the context of such anticipated developments as demographic trends and technical progress. Our comparison distinguishes three phases: a start-up phase, a "normal" phase, and an "end" phase, neglecting some economic side effects in the first step.

In the start-up phase, pay-as-you-go—in contrast to full funding—allows benefits to be paid immediately. This aspect was important in the United States after the Great Depression and in Switzerland in the late 1940s and early 1950s. To compare the two financing systems in a normal phase, one can first

look at the growth rate of total real wage income and at the real
interest rate. Between 1949 and 1978 the growth rate of total
wages in Switzerland exceeded the interest rate by 3.6 percentage points; this aspect favored the pay-as-you-go system. In
estimating the future performance of the two financing
systems, however, we must acknowledge that future growth
rates may be rather different. Because of increased life expectancy and a fall in the birthrate, there is widespread pessimism
about the effect of aging in the population. Increased life
expectancy, under both financing systems, means longer retirement periods and increased contributions. The decline in the
birthrate, however, harms the pay-as-you-go scheme more, as
it reduces the relative number of future workers available to
support future retirees. Unless the birthrate problem is offset
by technological progress, the performance of the pay-as-you-
go system will deteriorate (see table 4). The negative aspects of
pay-as-you-go become fully obvious if collective insurance has
to be reduced for some reason (end phase). With full funding,
less-serious problems occur.

As for the side effects, full funding—by inducing a higher
capital stock—will lead to higher marginal productivity of
labor and lower marginal productivity of capital. This effect
may be influenced, however, by government regulation and
investment policies which may distort the capital and real
estate markets. Moreover, since no direct relation exists between individual contributions and benefits in a pay-as-you-go
system, this method of financing is more appropriate to politically determined transfers.

The above arguments do not rule out a three-component
system partly based on pay-as-you-go financing and partly
funded. This follows from the three different lines of argument
presented. First, there is the usual reasoning in favor of collective compulsory insurance. Second, a comparison of the two
systems' direct costs on the basis of real internal rates of return
favors the pay-as-you-go system since—in Switzerland—the
growth rate of total real wage income exceeds the real interest
rate. Third, the economic side effects and the chain-letter char-

acter of the pay-as-you-go system favor full funding. Taking
into account the differences in economic data between the
United States and Switzerland, it is not surprising that we
reached totally different conclusions than Martin Feldstein
(1977, p. 24) did for the United States.

Present and future problems: a critical appraisal
of the three-component system

Basic program. We have seen that the basic component is both
an insurance scheme and a transfer program. Raising revenues
through payroll taxes and direct government contributions
conceals the program's redistributional effects and reduces
potential opposition.

Reform is hindered by the program's complexity and by the
privileges it offers certain groups. Some problems are obvious.
First, the share of government contributions is relatively arbitrary and varies over time (see table 2). There is a lower payroll
tax for self-employed people and supplementary reductions for
those with low incomes.[13] Further, to provide subsistence
benefits, supplementary payments are required in all cantons,
but many people who are entitled to them do not claim them
(cf., e.g., Schweizer 1980, pp. 68-70). Finally, as shown above,
the benefit formula favors people with higher than normal
income increases. This could be avoided by instituting a system
of calculations based on present values, or something similar.

In discussing the system's financial performance, we showed
that contributions to the basic program during the start-up
phase were used to give favorable treatment to the initial generation and to set up the trust fund, but that even during this
phase payroll taxes were supplemented by direct government
contributions. We also noted that for some high-income people
the present value of benefits exceeded the present value of contributions by a larger amount than is the case for low-income
people. An alternative procedure, which would avoid these inequities in the start-up phase, would provide minimum benefits
plus an amount determined by contributions. The latter
amount would at most return contributions with interest; i.e.,

the expected present value of additional benefits would never exceed the present value of additional contributions.[14] Such a formula would have permitted a temporary reduction in the payroll tax as well as the accumulation of a modest trust fund during the start-up phase.[15]

Supplementary program. In 1978 the supplementary program consisted of more than 17,000 institutions, voluntarily organized by private and public employers. Employees may lose a considerable part of their future claims if they change jobs. This creates strong ties between highly skilled employees and their firms, thus lowering mobility.

Planned extension of the supplementary program

The two houses of Parliament at present are drafting a bill to make the voluntary supplementary program mandatory in response to the 1972 constitutional amendment. This bill would extend the system of collective insurance, and the question now is how this extension will be financed. The pay-as-you-go basic component is popular partly because of the benefits it offers initial generations. It is also popular because of pessimism about the investment prospects for pension-fund reserves in funded systems—a pessimism which reflects concern over both present investment policies and anticipated government regulations.

On the other hand, full funding is attractive to those who foresee a decline in individual saving which would reduce the capital stock. Some people are anxious about demographic trends and about the chain-letter character of pay-as-you-go. Some people are even concerned about the possibility that a future initiative might ask for a reduction in the basic program.

The following institutional considerations (mainly unique to Switzerland) may influence the way the extension is organized. First, the beneficiaries of existing pension funds are afraid of a substantial loss if their funds are integrated into the new scheme. For this reason, and because of a general aversion to centralized bureaucracies, the present pattern of extreme decentralization is almost certain to provide the basic structure of any reformed system. Political forces also favor such an outcome, since such private financial institutions as life insurance companies have a strong interest in retaining a decentralized system which allows them to remain active in the pension-fund business.

The two bills now before Parliament propose using substantial elements of pay-as-you-go to finance the extended supplementary scheme. The Senate's version, which appears to have a better chance of enactment, proposes "age-dependent credits." This means that in one pension fund a constant proportion of members' wages would be credited to individual accounts according to the members' ages. An overall contribution of 15 percent thus would be credited to accounts within a range from 6 percent for the youngest employees to 22 percent for those within six years of retirement. Although payroll tax rates might vary among different institutions, within any one institution all would pay at the same overall rate. This clearly is a pay-as-you-go scheme, which means that an initial generation of beneficiaries would be heavily subsidized by younger workers. Beyond this basic structure, a relatively small contingency pool is planned. The investment behavior of pension funds will be determined by government regulations and by institutional characteristics.

Problems in the planned extension of the supplementary program

It has been argued that extending the supplementary program will have two effects. To begin with, it will reduce individual provision (the substitution effect). Second, the respective contributions are partly forced on individuals. If the extension is not largely financed by full funding, the capital stock will decline. Some people regard this as no serious problem. Yet increasing the capital stock may be important, considering the prospects for the Swiss economy in the international economic system—a small, open economy with few natural resources. In addition, wide agreement exists that there is no political necessity to favor another initial generation by using additional pay-as-you-go financing.

Age-dependent credits. The planned system of age-dependent credits will lead to discrimination against older workers if a pension fund is attached to a single firm, since such a firm can reduce the payroll tax by substituting younger workers.

There are two ways to avoid this. First, the pay-as-you-go financing within firm pension funds could be shifted to the national level. This would prevent discrimination, while retaining the politically desirable decentralization. Second, with slightly different implications, fixed employer contributions would avoid discrimination while variable employee contributions could take into account different incomes and household expenditures.

Investment behavior. Government regulations and institutional characteristics led to thinking in nominal terms—that is, without adjusting for inflation. In fact, despite the poor performance of bonds during the last two decades (cf. table 8), pension funds and life insurance companies mainly invest in nominal terms. Given government regulations, this behavior is perfectly rational. Because of the institutional climate, treasurers of pension funds have strong incentives to avoid wide fluctuations in economic performance; instead, they pursue strategies which yield more constant and predictable results. Nominal losses resulting from a slump in the stock market thus are considered worse than real losses on bonds stemming from inflation. For this reason, bonds and real estate have turned out to be prefered investments.

This discussion suggests that investment policies will not be reoriented towards objectives formulated in real terms. On the contrary, no expression such as "maintenance of real substance" appears in either of the two Parliament bills. It is even possible that more government controls may lead to more investment in nominal values as soon as the supplementary program becomes mandatory. If so, the result could be a substantial decline in the formation of risk capital. Furthermore, if investment in real terms should increasingly concentrate in real estate, distortions in this market could occur.

We have mentioned the possibility of a firm getting credit directly from its own pension fund. Suppose the firm is about to lay off part of its labor force because of cash-flow problems; the pension fund may then be willing to grant additional credit at a low interest rate, even if there is a high risk, in order to save some jobs. Since a centralized pool would cover serious pension-fund losses under the new bill, this risk would be less for the pension fund than for any other source. The pool could thus be used to maintain jobs in inefficient enterprises at the expense of the whole economy.

Some government regulations of investment policies may be necessary in order to deal with these problems. It would be appropriate for regulations to favor both the formation of risk capital and the maintenance of the real value of pension funds. This could be done, for instance, by restricting the deviations of the pension-fund portfolios from a combined stock-and-bond-market index.

Coordination between the basic and the supplementary programs

The basic program at present is a pay-as-you-go scheme, while the supplementary program is funded. The introduction of age-dependent credits now being proposed to extend the supplementary program would introduce a significant pay-as-you-go element into that program, thus reducing its total reserves. In an effort to clarify the relationships between the three components in the Swiss social security system, it would make sense to incorporate all pay-as-you-go features proposed for the supplementary program into the basic one, and then to organize the supplementary program on a purely funded basis. This would create a cleaner context within which to determine relative shares of the two programs and thus the amount of total reserves.

CONCLUSION

We have seen that the three-component concept seems to be appropriate to the Swiss context. But each component has its own particular problems.

The basic program has a complex structure. In start-up phases (introduction and extensions), some transfers occur which contradict the spirit of social security. Because of pay-as-you-go financing and unfavorable demographic trends, financial difficulties will emerge. The supplementary program in its present form consists of a highly decentralized pension-fund system which hinders mobility in the labor market. Investment policies for pension-fund reserves favor nominal values and—for the decade 1969-1978—they have yielded a real rate of return close to zero. When this program becomes mandatory, it seems unlikely that the current institutional difficulties will be overcome. Further, a special form of pay-as-you-go financing (age-dependent credits) will be introduced which could lead to discrimination in the labor market.

With respect to the third component, which is individual provision, there has been a sharp decline in the private saving rate in recent years which seems to have resulted partly from the expansion of mandatory insurance over the last decade. This development may be worrisome for the future economic growth of the Swiss economy. It is an important development in light of current deliberations over the question of how to finance extension of the supplementary program. In the end, the future growth of the Swiss economy may depend on financing extension of the supplementary program by a mechanism that is to a large extent funded.

8

SHERWIN ROSEN

United States

Social security and private pension plans. The 1935 Social
Security Act and its amendments. Mandatory participation.
Payroll taxes and benefit schedules—indexation. Inter-
generational transfers. Social security and saving behavior.
The work test and other disincentives. Inequities. Changing the
indexation method—bracket adjustment.

The U.S. social security program was established during the Great Depression in 1935 as a mandatory retirement program for the elderly, supplementing private insurance, saving, and pension plans. The program provides old-age and survivors' insurance covering retirees and dependents, disability insurance, and (since 1965) medical insurance for the aged and long-term disabled. Altogether, contributions to social security amounted to about 12.8 percent of gross national product (GNP) in 1978.

Organized as a pay-as-you-go system, the program is financed by a current (1981) payroll tax of 12.26 percent, split equally between employer and employee, on incomes up to $29,700. Eighty-eight percent of all covered worker earnings are thus taxable. Forty working quarters are necessary to establish eligibility for pensions, which are payable in full at age 65 and in a lesser amount at age 62. Benefits are based on average monthly indexed earnings (excluding the five lowest years in the average), with the scale of benefits "tilted" toward low-income earners. Benefits are indexed to increase in real income along with increases for inflation. Reforms enacted in 1977 will raise payroll taxes to 15.3 percent in 1990, and the ceiling will also rise with inflation.

Like the other countries surveyed in this book, the United States is experiencing a significant change in the age structure of its population because of a decline in the birthrate which began in the early 1960s. As a result, plausible extrapolations predict that the ratio of workers paying into social security to the number of beneficiaries will decline from a current value of 3.2 to 1.0 down to 2.0 to 1.0 in the year 2035 (see table 1, which shows the projected ratio of elderly to working-age population).

Table 1
Actual and Predicted Ratio[a] of Workers to Retirees in the U.S. Population by Year, 1960-2055

Actual		Projections					
			Ratio alternative[b]			Ratio alternative[b]	
Year	Ratio	Year	I	II	Year	I	II
1960	5.75	1985	4.95	4.90	2025	2.89	2.39
1965	5.49	1990	4.65	4.52	2030	2.65	2.10
1970	5.44	1995	4.44	4.22	2035	2.59	1.98
1975	5.29	2000	4.42	4.10	2040	2.63	1.91
1976	5.24	2005	4.44	4.02	2045	2.69	1.85
1977	5.24	2010	4.24	3.75	2050	2.67	1.75
1978	5.18	2015	3.77	3.27	2055	2.65	1.67
1979	5.15	2020	3.30	2.80			
1980	5.13						

Source: *1981 General Report of the Board of Trustees of Old-Age and Disability Insurance Trust Funds* (Washington, D.C.: U.S. Government Printing Office, 2 July 1981).

[a]This ratio is defined as the number of people aged 20-64 divided by the number of people in the population 65 years of age or older.

[b]Alternative I assumes an average fertility rate of 2.1 over the forecast period, while alternative II assumes an average fertility rate of 1.7. The recent average is 1.8. Alternative II also assumes an improvement in age-specific mortality experience over the forecast period that is twice as large as assumed for alternative I. See original source for more details. Note that the figures in this table do not make adjustments for secular changes in labor force participation rates and do not refer to the ratio of retirees to workers, but to the ratio of the elderly to the nonelderly. On the one hand there has been a trend toward earlier retirement, but on the other hand there has been an increasing trend of labor force participation of nonelderly women. These patterns of labor force participation are difficult to project.

The long-term funding problem was aggravated during the 1970s, when double indexation of benefits to inflation pushed the average replacement rate (benefits as a percentage of last earnings) from 31 percent in 1970 to 45 percent in 1978. While this error was corrected by the 1977 amendments, the long-term solvency of the program will require either reducing currently legislated benefits or increasing taxes to even higher levels. The precise extent of the problem depends on several things, including future economic growth and future fertility rates. Under the most pessimistic assumptions, payroll tax rates will have to rise to more than 26 percent in order to finance currently legislated benefits, and would have serious effects on incentives to work, save, and invest.

The effect on private saving has been much debated in the United States. Although there seem to be conflicting influences, the evidence shows some substitution of social security saving for private saving—thus reducing investment and economic growth. Agreement is limited, however, to the direction of this effect and does not extend to its size.

Effects on employment decisions come from two features of the work test. First, retirement benefits are subject to an earnings test and are reduced by $1 for each $2 above total income (wages plus benefits) of $5,500 per year. The earnings test has become relatively less important as the exempt amount has been increased. Returns on social security investment are also affected by choice of retirement age. Early retirement at 62 brings actuarial reductions in benefits from the normal retirement age of 65, but later retirement, after 65, does not bring an actuarially fair increase in benefits. These two features do create incentives which discourage work, though debate continues on the magnitude of the effect.

On transfer effects, the United States follows the normal pattern of transferring significant resources between generations, from the young to the old. As with all other countries, the largest transfers occurred for retirees during the start-up phase of the program, but the amounts transferred also varied with particular beneficiaries. The minimum transfer (to single retirees) is returning more than double contributions plus interest, and for some categories of beneficiaries the transfers run significantly more than that.

Transfers within generations are complex. While benefits are progressively tilted toward low-income people, the payroll tax is regressive, levied only on incomes up to a specified ceiling. Because social security is voluntary for some classes of employees (government and nonprofit-organization employees), some of the latter may establish eligibility for full benefits with relatively short contribution histories.

The law ignores actuarial distinctions; thus it discriminates in favor of women (who live longer than men) and against blacks (whose life expectancies are shorter than those of whites)—although the tilt of the benefit structure toward low-income people approximately cancels out the actuarial discrimination against blacks.

A final class of equity problems concerns the role of working spouses versus the unearned spouse benefit. The latter amounts to 50 percent of the worker's benefit when first claimed at age 65, regardless of work history. Recent increases in employment of married women has raised questions about the fairness of this system, which was established to support two-person, one-earner families.

The long-term funding problem may be solved either by increasing taxes or reducing benefits. Raising taxes does not seem viable either economically or politically. Reducing benefits, while politically difficult, could take the form of increasing the retirement age (which has been discussed) or of changing the indexation formula to accommodate only inflation. Either way, the sooner reforms are undertaken, the easier it will be to solve these long-term difficulties.

The question of how to finance the social security system, once one of the most popular pieces of legislation in the United States, was recently back in the headlines. To recall the background and history of this domestic public policy program and consider options for reform, this chapter explores the nature and economic consequences of social security as both an annuity system and an intergenerational tax transfer program. It examines the historical evolution of the program and its relation to the system we have today, as well as its current financial performance and future prospects; then it discusses the possible economic effects of the program on capital formation, labor supply, and income distribution. Finally, I suggest two modifications of existing law that will eliminate the long-run deficit: changing the indexation of benefits to a real purchasing-power concept rather than the relative-income concept written into the existing law, and extending eligibility for retirement benefits to a later age than 65, a proposal that otherwise leaves the present system intact. While there will continue to be extensive discussion about changing the retirement age, the possibilities for changing the indexation method have received far less attention, perhaps because this change is more difficult to understand. Nevertheless, it has much to recommend it. Though social security is in financial difficulties, the law can be amended in suitable and acceptable ways to maintain the system as our most important social legislation for many years to come.

BACKGROUND AND GENERAL SETTING

While workmen's compensation preceded the social security system by many years, the Social Security Act of 1935 was the first and most important comprehensive social insurance legislation in the history of the country.[1] The original act imposed payroll taxes, shared equally by employer and employee, on many classes of workers, and provided pension benefits to retired workers. Retirement annuities, however, were to be deferred until a largely funded reserve was built up. Thus the original Social Security Act was a form of mandatory saving which substituted government compulsion for individual initiative and self-reliance accomplished through voluntary saving and purchase of annuities in the private market.

The analogy of social security with private insurance was an important component of the original act, and that analogy continues today. Usually in discussions of social security this actuarial element is referred to as the "individual equity" of the system. The widespread social and economic disruptions of the 1930s, however, embedded other portions of the act in an aura of social welfare, involving the beginnings of an unemployment compensation system and aid to states for public assistance to the aged poor. Emphasis on income transfers and welfare aspects of social security, often called the "social adequacy" of the system, was and continues to be a source of tension with its individual equity aspects.

From the beginnings of social security in the United States, major differences of opinion regarding financing have been expressed and many of the same issues continue today. The Committee on Economic Security that outlined many features of the original act recommended partial general-revenue financing through the federal government. Congress, however, then cast a dim eye on that proposal and has continued to do so. An integral part of the program since its inception is the principle of basing individual retirement pensions from social security on prior covered earnings and prior payroll taxes, establishing claims as a matter of earned right and without a test of need. This feature, which stresses individual equity, is surely one of the reasons why social security (albeit with recent lapses) has been so popular.

If the principle of specific payroll taxes nominally shared by workers and employers has withstood assault over the years, elements of reserve funding initiated by the 1935 act quickly fell by the wayside in the major amendments of 1939. The date of annuity payments was advanced and benefit amounts were liberalized. Both of these changes started the program on a full pay-as-you-go basis, in which reserve funds were far less than obligations to current and future retirees. Further liberalization of eligibility and coverage in 1950 amendments, wherein large numbers of previously ineligible workers were blanketed-in upon nominal tax payments to the system, firmly instituted pay-as-you-go as the predominant method of financing. In 1940 the recommended reserve was approximately three years' expenses; but this has gradually eroded, so that today's actual reserves are even less than six months' anticipated outgo.

Under a pay-as-you-go system financed by payroll taxes, income does not accumulate in a fund or in each worker's individual account as it would in a private savings-retirement pension plan. Instead, virtually all income collected through taxes on existing workers is immediately paid out to current retirees, since the claims of each retiree are partially based on prior taxes paid into the system. U.S. social security hence is a curious mixture of both insurance and transfer elements—the former loosely approximated by the relation between taxes paid while working and benefits received during retirement, the latter a direct transfer through the payroll tax from those who are working to those who are retired. While the Social Security Administration over the years has made some rather misleading statements about the relation between individual taxes (euphemistically called "contributions") and reserves, Americans now widely understand that the reserves are purely for contingency purposes; they are merely meant to balance temporary departures between income and outgo, in much the same way that an individual holds reserve balances in a checking account to match irregular dating of receipts and expenditures.

The pay-as-you-go method of social security finance makes a person's rights under this system substantially different from those available in private pension-fund accounts. The latter provide much greater elements of voluntary choice; even though some firms require mandatory participation in pension plans, there is considerable variation among employers, and one may contribute even more to any given scheme on a roughly actuarial basis. The natural workings of the competitive market for labor induce firms to offer pension packages that cater to various types of workers; this alternative to wage competition also confers systematic income-tax advantages compared with direct monetary compensation, and it may be cheaper for firms to administer. Contributions accrue as individual claims to pension funds, and the proceeds are invested in various financial instruments, such as stocks and bonds, that represent claims to real capital goods. In other words, a private pension system is just a life-cycle manifestation of private saving and investment, often through the intermediary of one's employer. These claims are scarcely risk free; their value is subject to the normal risks of portfolio management and fluctuations in aggregate market valuations of capital in the economy. When claims are converted to annuities, moreover, the level of income that results depends on the market value of one's claims at that particular time. In light of the financial disasters of the 1930s, those carefully planning for retirement on the fruits of private savings accumulated in the 1920s unfortunately would have found their capital value far less than expected, compared to those who planned to retire when market values happened to be booming.

The reserve funding features built into the initial Social Security Act would have made the U.S. system somewhat comparable to the private system. There was considerable uncertainty about the desirability of funded versus unfunded pensions as is clear from the large changes in philosophy implicit in subsequent amendments. If a consensus had existed about full reserve funding, there would have been no particular reason for the federal government to directly involve itself in the pension business. A mandatory private-pension system could have been instituted using approved and certified private carriers with mandatory checkoffs from payrolls, in much the same way that workmen's compensation has been administered over the years.

There are good social reasons for mandatory participation in a pension scheme, of course, that are not necessarily anti-libertarian nor necessarily based on paternalistic views that a government knows more about what is best for its citizens than they do themselves. These concern the fact that unlucky or unwise individuals can and do throw themselves on the mercy of the state: fellow citizens do not knowingly allow people to starve in their old age. If this kind of implicit social "insurance," random though it may be, is available through private or public philanthropic organizations, incentives are provided for many people not to look into the future, to be less careful about their investments, and to be less prudent in their saving behavior—that is, it tends to promote those very instances where the mercy of the state must be invoked. Mandatory self-provision of a basic level of support is prudent social-policy action under these circumstances. There is perhaps no insurance scheme where the very act of insurance does not affect the probability of the hazardous event itself, since care and self-protection are good substitutes for market insurance; this is a manifestation of that general principle. Interaction with third parties through the good graces of the state—real external effects—provides an intellectual rationale for state involvement in these activities. Adherence to these classical principles of political economy, of course, says nothing about actual state provision of pensions rather than mandatory participation in the private sector and the questions of funded versus unfunded liabilities.

It is interesting that the pay-as-you-go, unfunded method of pension finance is generally held to be imprudent in the private sector—and indeed, is undesirable under U.S. law—because it does not, as a funded system does, divorce the financial fortunes of the firm from the value to its pension liabilities. The same difficulties, however, do not necessarily apply to the economy at large, because the prospects of the federal government's going bankrupt are not worth contemplating. The financial integrity of an unfunded social security system therefore depends on the power and willingness of the federal government to tax. In this sense the potential "fund" is the earning power of all current and future workers who can be taxed, its magnitude depending on the number and productivity of future workers. The claims of any individual on the system thus are not necessarily the tax-benefit schedules written into the law at any given time; the claims depend, rather, on the ability of Congress to tax members of the then working population during the time of one's retirement. Consequently, the legal status of these claims is entirely different from those of a private pension scheme. While the financial value of private claims is subject to considerable risk and uncertainty, claims on the public system have their uncertainties as well. That present law is not immutable and does not necessarily reflect one's real claims and obligations to the system is evidenced by the fact that Congress has amended the act more than a dozen times since 1937. Many of these amendments have involved significant benefit liberalizations. Benefits have grown in real terms, for example, by about 1 percent per year on average since 1940. These increases, however, have not come free; rather, they have come from correspondingly large increases in taxes, also provided by the amendments. On balance, it is clear that the *net* claims of each successive generation of retirees have fallen, and that they are likely to fall in the future.

Pay-as-you-go financing can be thought of as a "social compact" involving successive tax transfers across adjacent pairs of overlapping generations. The transfers go in one direction: from young to old. The fact that beneficiaries have made readily identifiable payroll-tax payments when young helps to "justify" retirement-transfer claims on the tax payments of the next generation. In a smoothly growing economy, with both population and productivity steadily rising, such a plan is feasible and easy to implement on a national scale. Yet there are major uncertainties. Population growth is notoriously erratic and difficult to predict, and productivity growth is subject to major fluctuations—such as the marked deceleration of the past decade—which are imperfectly understood. Since these form the bedrock on which unfunded pension liabilities rest, current events demonstrate their vulnerability to major tremors.

Given that social security did not go toward mandatory participation in private plans at a critical juncture—and surely the financial circumstances of the 1930s must have dampened the prospects of doing so—it is questionable whether funded governmental pensions are even feasible in the United States. Basically, there are two reasons for this.

The first concerns the control of politicians. Funds can be raided, and the temptation to do so arises because they are short-run alternatives to explicit and painful tax increases. When the latter might only occur more than a decade or two after a benefit increase and long beyond a politician's time horizon, the political gains to engage in such behavior are clear. A case can be made, in fact, that some of the benefit increases legislated in the 1960s were the direct result, through growth of the wage base, of unanticipated increases in revenues that were readily "spent" in this fashion. In the same vein, besides codifying the social compact across generations, most Americans are suspicious of expanding financing beyond earmarked payroll taxes to general revenues. This is because payroll taxes clarify the relation between benefit liberalizations and future tax costs and, through the political process, help to maintain better financial control of the system. General revenue finance breaks the link between income and outgo.

The second reason relates to political restrictions on how a fund of any magnitude can be held. Despite recent talk of "reindustrialization policies" and financial bailouts of major corporations, it is inconceivable that in the United States such a fund could be held in the form of private financial instruments and claims to private capital. These funds would therefore have to be held in U.S. government securities, but the ultimate value of government securities also rests on the government's power to tax and raise the real resources necessary to pay them off. In the present system, each person holds "implicit debt," as it were, in the form of promises to tax future generations. Explicit debt approximates the same type of claim, so whether this kind of financing would make a real difference compared to what we have now is a genuine question.

PERFORMANCE AND FINANCIAL PROSPECTS

The social security system in the United States today basically consists of three components: Old-Age and Survivors Insurance (OASI) covering retirees and dependents; Disability Insurance (DI); and, since 1965, Medical Insurance for the aged. All are financed by separate, earmarked payroll taxes equally levied on covered workers and on their employers. The economics of medical care and medical insurance is a topic large enough to warrant separate treatment, so attention focuses on the first two, abbreviated as OASDI.*

The prevailing social security concept is a three-tier system, with mandatory social security coverage providing the basic "rung" of support during oldage. Private supplements through individual initiative, participation in employer plans and the like, provide the upper layer of support, and the welfare system provides the lower layer of support for the aged poor. Coverage under the system has increased markedly over the years, so that more than 90 percent of all workers (including armed services personnel) are now included. To reflect its basic floor-of-support logic, not all earnings of covered workers are taxable. Rather, the law has always stipulated a maximum taxable earnings per worker, though this ceiling has gradually been raised over time; today more than 88 percent of covered workers' total earnings are taxable. The major classes of workers not now covered are employed in government sectors: most federal government workers are exempt, while state and local government workers and those employed by nonprofit institutions may voluntarily elect coverage. Many choose not to do so. Eligibility for the basic pension begins at age 65 (with reduction for early retirement beginning at age 62), so long as a person has forty quarters of covered earnings during working life. There are slightly different eligibility requirements for pensions to invalids incapable of gainful work.

Monthly retirement benefits are computed on the basis of average monthly indexed earnings, with exclusions dropping out five years of lowest covered earnings in the average. Monthly benefits increase with average earnings, but not proportionately. The benefit schedule is tilted in favor of those

---

*Perhaps because it is a very efficient public agency, at least as measured by the ratio of operating expenses to total disbursements, the Social Security Administration also oversees a wide variety of smaller and miscellaneous programs not discussed here.

with lower average earnings. Thus, even though the benefit amounts rise with average monthly earnings, the ratio of benefits to earnings falls as income rises. This nonproportionate schedule is supposed to reflect "social adequacy," and to that extent it departs from actuarial principles. Disability pensions have this characteristic, too. The system also gives allowances to dependents, such as 50 percent of a worker's pension paid to a spouse, widows' pensions, and death benefits. Benefits have been indexed since the early 1970s to allow for automatic cost-of-living adjustments associated with inflation.

Some basic program statistics are presented in table 2, which shows trends since 1937 and currently legislated tax schedules for the future. The first three columns show total payroll tax rates paid by a worker and his employer in each year, stated as percentages of taxable payroll: each of the worker's and employer's shares is one-half of these numbers. The fourth column shows the maximum taxable earnings base. This cannot be computed after 1982 because it will be determined by an indexation formula tied to future average covered wages. The four columns together show a rapid rate of tax increase. Some of the early increases in OASI taxes were natural outcomes of program maturity, since the beneficiary/worker ratio rose rapidly in those years. More recent tax increases reflect liberalization of benefits only, because little room exists for further increases in coverage.

The disability insurance tax shows an alarming rate of increase during the 1960s. This reflected an equally alarming increase of claims, an increase recently controlled by tighter program and claims monitoring. What these numbers do not show is that the overall size of the OASDI system has become very large relative to the public sector in the overall economy; it is second only to the general income tax in total taxes collected. For many people, social security payroll taxes exceed income tax payments.

Taxes are more easily summarized by their percentage rates than are benefits. The actual structure in law is a table showing how monthly benefits vary with average monthly earnings.

Table 2

Taxes and Benefits under Social Security

Year	Taxes				Monthly OASI benefits		
	Tax rate, total[a]			Maximum taxable earnings	Maximum benefit[b]		Replacement rate[d]
	Total	OASI	DI		Year of retirement	1980	
1937	2.0	2.00	—	$3,000			
1950	3.0	3.00	—	3,000	$45.2	$316.4	.19
1954	4.0	4.00	—	3,600	85.0	349.5	.34
1960	6.0	5.50	.50	4,800	119.0	395.6	.33
1966	8.4	7.00	.70	6,600	132.7	412.1	.30
1970	9.6	7.30	1.10	7,800	189.8	453.4	.31
1975	11.7	8.75	1.15	14,100	316.3	515.4	.40
1978	12.1	8.55	1.55	17,700	459.8	615.2	.45
1979	12.26	8.67	1.50	22,900	503.4	632.5	
1980	12.26	8.67	1.50	25,900	572.0	653.8	
1981	13.3	9.05	1.65	29,700			
1982-84	13.4	9.15	1.65	—[c]			
1985	14.1	9.50	1.90	—[c]			
1986-89	14.3	9.50	1.90	—[c]			
1990+	15.3	10.20	2.20	—[c]			

Sources: *Social Security Bulletin*, Annual Statistical Supplement; *1980 Trustee Report of Social Security Trust Funds*; Munnell 1979.

[a]These rates are the sum of employer and employee rates. The total rate shown is the sum of Old-Age and Survivors Insurance, Disability Insurance, and Hospital Insurance.

[b]Refers to men only, for retirement at age 65.

[c]Subject to automatic provisions under indexation formula.

[d]For worker retiring at age 65 with average earnings.

Table 2 shows maximum benefits available to a worker upon retiring in selected years. It also shows what these amounts would have paid off in 1980, given the many amendments and inflation adjustments made over the years. A large increase from the late 1960s to the late 1970s is especially notable in both columns. The average person, of course, does not qualify for the maximum benefit, but these figures at least show the general trend. Probably the best single measure of benefits is the replacement rate, which is the ratio of annual scheduled benefits to average covered earnings just before retirement (see the last column of table 2). It is clear that no deep principle underlies this particular ratio, because earnings vary greatly over the life cycle and it does not take account of unearned income. Nevertheless, it is easy to understand, and it is also useful for indicating basic trends. The table shows that the replacement rate for the average worker ranged from .30 to .35 for most of the program's history, with a precipitous increase to .45 in the last ten years—an increase consistent with the benefit explosion noted in the other columns.

This explosion of benefits has been caused by a precipitous rise in the inflation rate over the past decade and a half and—quite unintentionally—by changes in the Social Security Act designed to deal with that problem. Several legislative changes in the late 1960s and early 1970s increased benefits to take account of inflation, but the inflationary environment developed so rapidly that in 1972 it was thought desirable to provide automatic increases analogous to escalator clauses for cost-of-living adjustments in wage contracts. The benefit formulae and provisions of social security are far too complicated, however, to be made inflation-proof by a simple cost-of-living adjustment, and the 1972 indexation amendments in reality accomplished nothing new; they had been done before on an *ad hoc* basis. The old *ad hoc* indexation methods allowed quicker reactions to adverse (or favorable) data feedback from program-operating statistics. The automatic method was—and was meant to be—more rigid in that respect. What's more, a serious technical error in the indexation adjustments was written into the 1972 amendments, an error so serious that, given the price and wage inflation of the middle 1970s, the benefit system was literally out of control.

Errors built into the system probably resulted from lack of experience with inflationary adjustments in U.S. social programs; while the error seems obvious in retrospect, it is easy to see how it was made at the time. Although details are complicated, the basic problem was that the formula linked the entire benefit/average-monthly-earnings schedule with the inflation rate. Hence, the inflation did two things to the benefit computation. For a given schedule, it raised one's average earnings and therefore increased benefits. In addition, it raised the entire schedule itself and thereby raised benefits even more. As a result, real benefit levels and replacement rates were tied, irrationally and illogically, to the rates of price and wage inflation themselves. The procedure tended to make a double adjustment for inflation rather than a single one, so that benefit claims increased much faster than the inflation rate. This technical error probably accounts for the marked rise in replacement rates shown in table 2 and for the great increase in real benefits during these years. A more rational indexing method instituted in the 1977 amendments finally corrected this error and brought benefits under control.

The constellation of benefits rising at a much faster rate than taxes led to a steep decline in social security trust funds in the mid-1970s. It was clear that the situation could not continue without danger of short-run insolvency. The 1977 amendments not only indexed benefits more rationally, but they raised taxes to a level deemed sufficient to rescue the system. But any short-run accounting of social security revenues and payments must rest on projections of productivity, labor force participation, and the like. In retrospect, the mid-1970s' projections for the present state of the economy were too optimistic; as a result, the social security system is again in jeopardy.

Table 3 summarizes the near-term data. Actuaries use three sets of assumptions in making these imputations, based on varying projections about economic factors such as rates of recovery, unemployment, and higher inflation in the next few years. By any of these measures, the short-run outlook is unfavorable; the OASI fund is likely to be exhausted within the coming year because the 1977 amendments did not foresee the poor economic performance of the economy in the last three years. Stagflation has produced falling real wage rates and more inflation than anticipated. Benefits to existing retirees

Table 3

Trust Fund Ratios Projected to 1984

Assumptions	Fund at 1 January as a percent of outgo during year					
	1979	1980	1981	1982	1983	1984
Optimistic:						
OASI[a]	30	23	15	8[b]	2	— 4
OASI and DI[a] combined	30	24	19	15	12	11
OASI, DI, and HI[a] combined	34	29	24	24	24	26
Intermediate:						
OASI	30	23	15[b]	6	— 2	—10
OASI and DI combined	30	24	18	12	8[b]	4
OASI, DI, and HI combined	34	29	24	21	19	18
Pessimistic:						
OASI	30	23	14[b]	3	— 9	—21
OASI and DI combined	30	24	18	9[b]	0	— 8
OASI, DI, and HI combined	34	29	23	18	11[b]	5

Source: Summary of the *1980 Trustee Report of Social Security Trust Funds*.

[a]OASI (Old-Age and Survivors Insurance), DI (Disability Insurance), HI (Hospital Insurance).

[b]Fund(s) become unable to pay benefits during this year. Ratios for later years are theoretical.

have therefore grown rapidly with cost-of-living escalation, but the tax base, because of slow productivity growth and high unemployment rates, has not kept pace.

Disability (DI) and hospital insurance (HI) funds are in much better shape than OASI, so the combined status of all three together is more favorable than that of OASI alone. Congress recently combined these funds—a form of interfund borrowing which should guarantee payments for the next year or two without further legislation. Since, as explained above, "trust funds" in these accounts are merely contingency reserves, no serious contentions about the nature of social security are involved in this combination. The law of averages, in fact, suggests greater overall reserve-contingency value from pooling because the demands on each account are not perfectly correlated. Even so, it is likely that the system will need outside support within a few years unless the economy makes a remarkable and improbable recovery. Statistical theory suggests that periodic difficulties of a contingency-reserve system are inevitable unless the reserve is much larger than it has recently been. Short-term borrowings from the treasury to balance macroeconomic fluctuations outside the system's control are not unreasonable as solutions to this short-run problem. The same principles are involved as with personal finance, where loans that are soon to be repaid can effectively transfer income from better times to temporary periods of stringency by temporary borrowing and subsequent repayment.

If the short-term prospects of social security look bleak, they pale next to the long-run prospects. The fundamental problem lies in the much-discussed change since the early 1950s in U.S.—and worldwide—demographic trends. The great baby boom of the 1950s was followed by a baby dearth which occurred simultaneously with other significant social and demographic changes: rapid increases in female labor force participation and marked increases in marital instability. There are currently approximately 3.2 workers for each beneficiary in the United States; forty years from now there may be only 2.0 workers for each beneficiary. Since social security is an intergenerational transfer system which taxes the working population and transfers the proceeds to the retired, the cause for concern is evident. The wage base will inevitably shrink relative to the size of the aging population to be supported.

Some of the relevant data is in table 4. Again, various economic and demographic assumptions underlie these projections, and the potential forecast error becomes larger for periods further away in time. For example, the adult population can be well predicted for the next twenty years because most people who will then be adults have already been born. A fifty-year projection requires forecasts of birthrates and immigration in

Table 4

Estimated Average Annual Expenditure of OASDI System under Alternative Assumptions and Comparison with Average Scheduled Tax Rate
(as percent of taxable payroll)

Calendar years	Average scheduled tax rate	Estimated average expenditure by alternative[a]			Difference by alternative		
		I	II	III	I	II	III
OASI[b] (retirement):							
1980-2004	9.83	8.81	9.42	10.35	1.02	.41	— .52
2005-2029	10.20	10.16	11.92	14.83	.04	—1.72	— 4.63
2030-2054	10.20	11.36	15.37	24.50	—1.16	—5.17	—14.30
1980-2054	10.08	10.11	12.24	16.56	— .03	—2.16	— 6.48
DI[b] (disability):							
1980-2004	2.02	1.10	1.24	1.38	.92	.78	.64
2005-2029	2.20	1.32	1.65	2.00	.88	.55	.20
2030-2054	2.20	1.23	1.61	2.10	.97	.59	.10
1980-2054	2.14	1.22	1.50	1.83	.92	.64	.31
Total:							
1980-2004	11.85	9.91	10.66	11.73	1.94	1.19	.12
2005-2029	12.40	11.48	13.57	16.84	.92	—1.17	— 4.44
2030-2054	12.40	12.59	16.98	26.60	— .19	—4.58	—14.20
1980-2054	12.22	11.33	13.74	18.39	.89	—1.52	— 6.17

Source: Summary of *1980 Trustee Report of Social Security Trust Funds.*

[a]Alternative I is optimistic; alternative II is intermediate; alternative III is pessimistic.

[b]OASI (Old-Age and Survivors Insurance), DI (Disability Insurance).

the next twenty years, and these are difficult to ascertain. The optimistic assumptions (labeled I) project greater real wage growth, lower unemployment and inflation rates, and more favorable demographics, while the pessimistic assumptions

(III) have the opposite characteristics. Intermediate assumptions (II) are compromises between the two.

Table 4 shows both average scheduled tax rates under current law and estimated average annual obligations in comparable units for the next three twenty-five-year periods. Differences between tax rates and expenditure/payroll ratios indicate surpluses or deficits. The table clearly shows a deficit of major proportions in the existing set-up; it began to appear within two decades after the turn of the century, and it gets progressively worse thereafter. Even under the intermediate assumptions, the scheduled tax rates must rise eventually to more than 18 percent of taxable payroll in order to balance the long-run budget; under the pessimistic assumptions, tax rates must rise to more than an astounding 25 percent of the taxable payroll. Put in another way, alternative III projections show that social security disbursements will rise from less than 5 percent of the present gross national product (GNP) to 9 percent by the middle of the next century. Per-worker expenditure shares will rise even more because of the demographics. Since each percent of payroll now represents more than $10 billion per year and substantially more than that in later years, the numbers in table 4 give one pause. The long-run deficit, even allowing for discounting to present value, is in the neighborhood of $1 trillion or more. The enormous size of these numbers is sure to have substantial impact on the economy.

SOCIAL SECURITY AND THE ECONOMY

Three important areas of interaction between social security and the economy are subject to increasing scrutiny by economists. Professional interest in these matters seems to be proportional to the size of the social security budget. The three issues are: the relation between social security and private capital formation, its effect on retirement patterns, and its effect on income distribution and inequality. Each of these problems is so large and complex that only the major issues can be briefly reviewed here.[2]

Social security and private capital formation

To study saving behavior, economists use an apparatus based on the theory of rational decision-making over the life cycle. Apart from short-run contingency savings—which need not concern us—personal savings play two main roles in a person's life. One is to transfer income among members of the family, especially to dependents, as investments in education, bequests, and the like; the other is to transfer income across time periods in one's own life. People save money during working years in anticipation of dissaving to support their retirement.

From the private point of view, any asset which promises future income is equally satisfactory to transfer income across periods. One alternative is financial instruments which represent claims on the earning power of real capital assets; claims to social security income are another. Although social security is not funded, taxes paid by the individual or on his behalf have much the same effect as other acts of individual saving because they "buy" a claim to future income during retirement. No matter that this claim is backed by government taxing power rather than by the income-producing power of real capital; a dollar is a dollar.

The inherent substitution between these assets in private saving decisions is even closer. Social security taxes can actually yield a rate of return comparable to the interest paid by ordinary financial instruments. For the economy at large, this return is supported by expanding population and productivity. Given steady population growth and a constant ratio of retirees to workers, for example, a constant tax rate applied to an ever-growing wage base yields ever-increasing benefits for successive generations of retirees. Each person's taxes are smaller than his subsequent benefits, because the latter are paid by a larger and more productive population. Unfortunately, the changing demographics in a sense have reduced this "rate of return" for the baby-boom generation, as indicated by the system's long-term deficit. On this ground alone, mandatory social security saving should reduce private saving. The main difference is that one is funded and the other is not; one accumulates real capital and the other does not.

The problem is not quite so simple, however. The work test of social security may induce earlier retirement, and the necessity to produce an income over a longer period of retirement may well encourage private saving during working life. In this case, more social security and private saving are complements rather than substitutes.[3]

Social security operates within an extensive, private, intergenerational transfer system, especially in the family. To the extent that working children previously supported their retired parents, increased social security benefits should reduce private transfers. The trend in living arrangements of the elderly indicates this. The same thing would also be true in the opposite direction: increasing the tax burden of children by increasing benefits to their parents would be offset by even larger bequests. Note that without bequests, the life-cycle theory implies no net capital accumulation over the lifetime. Private savings when young are dissaved when old in either case. Hence if social security pays competitive rates of return, it does not affect an individual's net life-cycle wealth and does not affect total life-cycle saving.[4] In this respect, private saving and social security saving are equivalent, though the transition effects represented by building up assets and working them down in oldage are substantially different.

In summary, there are many effects of social security on private saving, not all in the same direction. Direct study of private offsets has been hampered by a serious lack of data on private intergenerational transfers and, in most studies, by the sensitivity of research results to empirical specifications, data periods, and definitions. Consequently, the estimates are not as sharp as one might hope. Yet the main evidence reveals some substitution of social security saving for private saving so that the private capital stock is therefore smaller. There is, however, no consensus on its magnitude. Despite claims of capital shortages in the U.S. economy, little direct evidence to that effect has been produced. To the extent that capital shortfalls exist, there is a tendency for the rate of return on capital to rise and to stimulate greater investment. This indirect effect must be smaller than the initial impact effect of social security, but it may not be trivial. In any case, it serves to offset the asset-substitution effect.

Effects on retirement

Though social security in the United States has been based on a program of earned entitlements without a test of need, it has always used a work test. Loose talk connects payments with "retirement insurance," yet both logic and common sense suggest that insurance is not feasible in this instance because individuals have so much control over their eventual retirement. The presence of the work test must therefore go to the origins of the act itself in the 1930s, when work effort was positively discouraged. More than a dozen amendments over the years, changing the test, reveal a deep ambivalence about its desirability.

There are two general features of the work test in present law. First, benefits for recipients under 72 years of age are reduced by $1 for each $2 above $5,500 per year—an implicit 50 percent tax rate on earned income above that amount. The exempt amount has risen significantly in recent years, making the test less stringent. It will be made even less stringent in the future. Second, eligibility for the basic pension is geared to age 65, with early retirement options at reduced annual benefits going down to age 62. These reductions are almost actuarially fair, in that expected present discounted values are approximately constant between ages 62 and 65. Deferring retirement beyond age 65 increases annual benefits, but at actuarially unfair rates. Benefit increases after age 65 do not accumulate sufficient interest to maintain capital values if retirement is postponed; consequently, postponing retirement beyond that age is implicitly taxed in the existing system. Earlier retirement is not discouraged either. Since social security benefits are exempt from income taxation, the structure in fact may actually encourage early retirement. Furthermore, the work test penalizes work beyond a certain amount, given that one is receiving benefits. It is ironic that these features tend to discriminate against those who have invested most heavily in human capital and for whom earnings capacity is their major income-producing asset—namely, the aged poor.

There is no doubt that disincentives to working are built into the benefit structure. How effective are they? Here the time-series data show enormous declines in labor-force participation of the aged in the period after World War II and a great increase in early retirement in the last decade. Furthermore, life expectancy of the aged has increased since the 1930s, so that the period for receiving benefits has increased significantly over the years. Detailed studies show similar effects.[5] They find that illness is a major cause of retirement, a fact which partially justifies the retirement "insurance" view; but they also find plenty of discretionary influences on retirement, including the effects of pension eligibility. An interesting development in this line of research links savings and retirement decisions in a life-cycle contest, since these are simultaneous decisions. Finally, if social security has indeed discouraged work activity among the elderly, it has also discouraged development of jobs that cater to their work habits and leisure preferences—part-time, part-year work, and so forth—thereby making empirical detection of work-restriction effects especially difficult.

Issues of equity and inequality

In a program as complicated as social security, certain inequities are inevitable. Still, they should be minimized. This complex subject is so tied to specific details of the law as to render any simple summary almost impossible.[6] Many problems, however, are created by tension between actuarial and welfare points of view. There are three main sources of difficulty.

(i) The benefit schedule gives higher replacement rates to the poor and therefore appears to be progressive, yet the nonproportional payroll tax is regressive. A simple reconciliation is to compute the implicit rate of return on social security taxes, a rate which historically has been comparable to market-interest rates for those fully covered by the system. It was, of course, much larger for those blanketed into the system in the earlier years, for their taxes were only a small fraction of the full amount. As already noted, returns will be lower for many future generations of retirees. Social security definitely has not been neutral between different generations.

There are more easily remedied inequities as well. The tilted benefit schedule, for example, works to the advantage of those with briefer histories of covered earnings because they look poor, yet many individuals qualifying on this basis are not poor at all. Some received government pensions at a relatively early age, and subsequently worked the minimum number of quarters in covered employment to become eligible for social security pensions as well. This good deal from social security encourages the practice of ''double dipping,'' and it demonstrates an abuse caused by nonmandatory participation. The only solution will be universal coverage, and this proposed reform has received much nonpartisan support.

(ii) The law ignores many actuarial distinctions, so that the rate of return varies unfairly across demographic groups. For example, women have much longer life expectancy than men and blacks have less life expectancy than whites. Other things being equal, this increases the return for women and decreases it for blacks. These issues are more complicated, however, because income patterns differ among these groups. For instance, it has been found that the tilted benefit schedule favors the lower average covered earnings of blacks as much as worse mortality experience disadvantages them, so the two effects approximately cancel each other out.

(iii) Serious and important issues arise from the fact that

social security calculations of costs and benefits are based on different accounting units. Cost accounting is done on an individual basis, but benefit calculations use the family as the fundamental unit. These issues were not significant in the early days, but the law has not kept pace with recent changes in the structure of families and in female labor-force participation. The greatest problem at present is the spouse's benefit; this amounts to 50 percent of the husband's benefit irrespective of work history. It was originally meant to increase support for two-person, one-earner families of retirees, until recently the predominant type. (A spouse may, of course, be eligible for higher benefits if warranted by her covered earnings record.) Two inequities are created by this. First, many married women who work, but who do not earn enough to be eligible for a greater single-worker benefit, merely subsidize the system and put two-earner families at a disadvantage compared with one-earner families. As female labor-force participation has risen, this issue has become increasingly important. Second, housewives have no direct right to benefits, and the increase in divorce has strained the system's ability to protect these people; a wife loses claim to a spouse benefit in the event of divorce if the marriage has not lasted for ten years, which enforces a dependency that is inconsistent with modern views of marriage and of the role of women in society.

The only proper resolution of these thorny issues is to use the same unit of account for costs and benefits. So many women are working today that switching to an individual unit of account for both is an interesting possibility to consider. Family units with earnings-sharing features, however, have some virtues, too. There are no perfect solutions to these problems, but surely a better solution can be found than present practice.

WHAT CAN BE DONE?

A rather bleak picture has emerged of an unfunded pension system potentially out of control, in deep short-run and long-run financial difficulty, exerting powerful adverse influences on capital accumulation and labor force decisions, with significant inequities built into it. Nevertheless, social security has been and probably remains one of the most popular of all government programs. The reason is that, although it is a transfer from young to old, each person in a sense "buys" the right to benefits by virtue of having been taxed while young. Given these implicit obligations to the current working generations, there is no question that they cannot be repudiated. Some form of the current system must be maintained, and reforms can realistically be made only within the context of the existing structure.

Many long-term reforms—such as removal of the work test, using individual units of account, taxing some benefits under the income tax, and so forth—can do much to eliminate adverse incentive effects and to make the system more equitable. The overriding issue that must be addressed immediately, however, is the system's poor financial status. So far as this author is aware, deficits can be dealt with in only two ways: either income must be increased or expenditure reduced. This is an unfortunate fact of economic life.

For the short run, it remains to be seen how effective the attempted solution of temporarily combining the reserve funds of OASI, disability, and hospital accounts will prove to be. If the economy does not recover rapidly, temporary borrowings from the treasury may be necessary. On the expenditure side, short-term problems are caused by the fact that in the last couple of years indexation of benefits through the price index rose 3 or 4 percentage points more than nominal wages. Real standards of living of those paying taxes are falling temporarily, while living standards of beneficiaries are being maintained. To what extent should retirees and not currently productive workers be immune to short-run macroeconomic fluctuations in the economy at large? Since private savings balances are hardly immune from fluctuations in capital value, at least some social security risks should be shared by both workers and retirees. A possible way to do this is to index existing benefits by the lower range of the price index or the wage index so that inflation could make current benefit payments rise no more rapidly than wages.

For the longer term, the impending tax burden caused by our recent demographic changes is so onerous that there will be no alternative to reducing social security's obligations under the law. We must face up to the fact that benefits now promised to future retirees must be reduced to more manageable levels. As noted previously, the replacement rate has risen in the last fifteen years by more than one third. It must be reduced toward its historically lower average in the future.

This is not as difficult a problem as it might seem. The current benefit schedule and the indexation adjustments enacted in the 1977 amendments have been written to maintain the replacement ratio of all future retirees at its current high level. However, the forces of economic growth, technical change, and capital accumulation virtually guarantee that the long-run lifetime earnings of future retirees will be larger than those of current and previous retirees. Just as we as a generation are, on average, wealthier than our parents and grandparents, so too will our children and their children be wealthier than we are. Therefore, maintenance of the replacement rate at its current high level means that the actual real dollar amount of benefits is promised to rise for these future wealthier generations. The simplest way to cure the long-term deficit is to change the law in such a way that the level of real benefits is held constant, at least for a time, and not to allow it to rise with increases in the general standard of living. This would not reduce anyone's benefits below what people are receiving now, adjusted for inflation. Instead, it would eliminate promised increases in real benefits in excess of current levels, which increases probably cannot be financed in any event. Furthermore, when the replacement rate has fallen to a more appropriate level, the law can be changed to maintain it there as circumstances warrant.

There are many ways in which this reduction can be accomplished. A detailed proposal would require tedious discussion of indexation schemes, which the reader will be spared. My own preference is to basically maintain the existing system, but not to fully index the bracket levels in the benefit schedule—only to index them in part. With the continued inflation of the past few years, this will gradually reduce the replacement rate—and hence all obligations of the system to future retirees—down to more appropriate levels. It is important to understand that this will not change the obligations to any current retirees, nor to future retirees once they have begun receiving benefits. It will only change the computation of the initial benefit amounts, which will thereafter be indexed to maintain their purchasing power. Much confusion in the present debate on indexation would be avoided by understanding the crucial difference between initial benefit indexation and subsequent benefit indexation. While indexing subsequent benefits to prices rather than to wages would clearly help resolve the short-term deficit, the solution to the long-term deficit lies in reducing the initial benefit computation.

In fact, adopting this change in indexing methods would practically remove the long-term deficit by itself.[7] But there is much more to recommend it. It would cause no absolute deterioration of benefits; they would only fall *relative* to increasing real income over time. This is consistent with the general principle of social security, which is meant to provide a basic floor of support for the elderly. It stands to reason that the floor should be maintained in real terms, while self-reliance is encouraged as people become wealthier. As an added bonus, the new indexation method would promote private thrift and reduce whatever impact social security exerts over private capital formation. This relative winding down of the system would also help with other structural problems, such as the disincentives for working.

The history of amendments to the Social Security Act clearly shows that there are no barriers to raising real benefits when it is thought desirable; Congress has done this a dozen times or more already. However, it is only fair that they be raised openly by law, rather than concealed in an arcane indexing formula. It is important to reemphasize that this indexing change would take no real purchasing power from future beneficiaries once they have begun to receive benefits, but would reduce initial benefit calculations to the extent that benefits are only partially indexed for future inflation. There is nothing in the principles and purposes of social security to impede this change, which reflects the same practical logic as the removal of double indexing from benefit calculations in 1977; it is not in the public interest to promise benefits that will prove extremely difficult—if not simply impossible—to deliver.

A second reform approach would be to gradually raise the retirement age. The drop in average retirement ages and increase in average longevity over the years has increased average retirement by 30 percent or more. As we have seen, the system itself has probably encouraged the early retirement part of this increase. Several countervailing forces, however, are promoting a longer work life. Not only do people live longer, but the quality of life among the elderly has improved generally, so more of them are able and willing to work. Furthermore, the increased popularity of higher education has deferred entry into the labor force to later ages, and work is not as physically demanding and unhealthy as it used to be. The recent increase in the age of mandatory retirement testifies to this trend. Since the impact of this sort of reform is more severe the older one is, it would have to be implemented gradually and with great care.

WEIGHING THE OPTIONS

Growing awareness of the social security system's financial difficulties has led to increasing public debate on possible solutions. While no clear consensus has as yet emerged, there appears to be considerable political support for raising the retirement age. This option may be the more popular simply because indexation reform is relatively difficult to understand. Both methods effectively reduce benefits. For future retirees, there are substantial differences between the two, however. Postponing benefits while maintaining the present indexation formula also maintains the relative status of benefits during fewer retirement years. Changing the indexation formula to wind down the replacement rate while maintaining the current eligibility age maintains the absolute position of payments at present levels, but with inflation and/or economic growth it allows them to decline *relative* to higher future earnings.

It is not clear which proposal is more equitable or which will be chosen. Extending the retirement age, however, will probably lead to greater difficulties in the long run because, as the standard of living rises, people tend to retire earlier, not later; and the reform thus conflicts with people's natural desires to consume more leisure as their incomes rise. On the other hand, freezing absolute benefits does not at all preclude increasing them later, if experience warrants, and also promotes greater individual initiative through the private sector.

The social security system has proved remarkably durable, and despite its serious financial difficulties there is no question that it can be successfully reformed. It is time for the social security problem to be solved.

9

KARL HEINZ JÜTTEMEIER
HANS-GEORG PETERSEN

West Germany

The present federal system and subsystems—general, special, industrial. Increased benefits and contributions. Demographic problems. Pensions and private saving. Funding or financing. Taxes, contributions, and work disincentives. Redistribution. Solutions to labor-market problems.

West Germany has three principal sources of retirement income: the state pension system, private firms' pension plans, and individual life insurance. In the state system, a basic mandatory program covers most employees, but the program is voluntary for the self-employed. Pensions paid from the compulsory general public system amounted to about 11.2 percent of gross national product (GNP) in 1977, which compared with much smaller payments from pension plans of private firms (1.3 percent in 1977) and from private life insurance (1.6 percent). Special programs also exist for other groups, including government officials, farmers, and war victims.

The general government retirement program is financed on a pay-as-you-go basis, partly by a payroll tax usually divided equally between employers and employees, and by a transfer from general revenues—a transfer which has been declining in recent years; in 1981 it is expected to cover about 14.0 percent of total program costs. The payroll tax amounts to 18.5 percent of gross wages up to a ceiling of DM 52,800 ($22,176 U.S. at an exchange rate of DM = $0.42 U.S. as of 1 July 1981). Pensions are normally payable at age 65; but men at age 63 and women as well as unemployed men at 60 may elect early retirement with no loss of benefits, but with an earnings test which applies only to early retirement.

Individual pensions depend on contributions, on the number of pensionable years, and on the relative income position during total working life. For several reasons, the average working life of men is greater than that of women (38 years for men versus 25 for women in 1977), and men therefore have higher pensions in relation to last earnings (replacement rate) than women (57.0 percent for men, 37.5 percent for women). Since 1957 pensions have been indexed to reflect both inflation and real income growth.

Funding problems first appeared in the mid-1960s, when expenditures began to exceed revenues. The government responded by raising the payroll tax rate from 14 percent in 1967 to 18 percent in 1973. In 1972, however, it also made the system considerably more generous. During the recession, which began in 1974, it became clear that the system was faced with a financial crisis, and in 1978 the government implemented a series of reductions in outgo. A further reduction is planned for 1983.

Looking to the future, the ratio of workers to retirees (excluding the public pensions for *Beamte*) will remain fairly constant until 1990, declining from 2.19 in 1980 to an estimated 2.11 in 1990. After that, however, following the experience in other countries, the ratio will decline significantly to 1.56 in 2010 and to an incredible 1.12 in 2030. The extent of the problem may be realized by considering that the number of employed personnel could decline by 30 percent in the period between 2000 and 2030.

These changes would cause a serious financial strain on the system, such that—under certain reasonable assumptions—payroll taxes would have to be increased from 18.5 percent to 32.0 percent in order to maintain currently legislated benefits in 2030. Reduced assumptions about economic growth would make the problem still worse.

The long-term financial outlook is aggravated by an extremely generous pension formula which links pensions to gross wages but does not tax them. Since it is possible to cumulate pension benefits from different pension sources, net benefits for individual pensioners frequently equal more than 100 percent of the last wage, after tax.

There is no conclusive evidence that the pension system has reduced saving in West Germany, whose payroll tax and saving rates are both among the highest in the world.

On employment effects, until 1972 there was no earnings test and thus no effect on employment. But provisions for early retirement enacted in that year impose a 100 percent tax on benefits above monthly wages of DM 1,320 ($554.40 U.S.) for pensioners who retire at age 63, and on benefits above DM 550 monthly earnings ($231.00 U.S.) for people who retire at 60. In the longer term, rising payroll-tax rates combined with a general rise in taxation may well prod many people either to avoid employment or to join the underground economy.

Since net pensions have been increasing faster than net wages, redistribution from workers to pensioners has become a live political issue. There are also redistributive effects within generations. Elements of the pension system tend to favor retirees with low pensions, government officials, and the self-employed, whereas certain tax regulations tend to favor the rich. Since the tax and transfer systems are not coordinated, their net redistributive impact is far from clear.

Recent official reports have suggested measures to relieve the economy of the burden imposed by the pension system. But incremental solutions will not be enough in the long term. A fundamental change is needed in the prevailing attitudes of politicians and the public so that they will no longer expect a paternalistic state to produce an endless stream of benefits.

DEVELOPMENT AND STRUCTURE OF THE CURRENT SYSTEM

In retrospect, one of the most creditable achievements of the Bismarck era was probably the introduction of a social security system which remained largely unchanged despite the economic and political disruptions of later German history. The system enjoys a unique popularity. For roughly one fifth of the

West German population, social security provides the major source of income, and this proportion will increase in the years to come.

Yet despite its success, social security is becoming more and more subject to criticism, and there is a growing awareness of future problems. The introduction in 1957 of annual pension adjustments as well as 1972 measures which greatly liberalized benefits have severely strained the retirement insurance system. With today's pension formula, dramatic demographic developments at the end of the century will enormously increase expenditures. In the current political climate, measures are often discussed which could impair the future growth potential of the West German economy and thus make future solutions even more difficult. Because social retirement insurance cannot be reformed overnight, a long-term perspective must be found which does not impose a hopeless burden on current or future working generations.

Today's social security is the outcome of nearly a century of experience, which began with the emperor's message on 17 November 1881. The next eight years brought public health insurance (1883), industrial injuries insurance (1884), and disability and retirement pension insurance (1889). In its original design, Bismarck's retirement insurance was a funded system which followed the pattern of ordinary private insurance:[1] risk sharing among individuals, with contributions paid according to the probability of the insured event. But even these early systems had redistributive features.

In 1948 superinflation and monetary reform almost completely destroyed the social insurance funds (and those of private insurance companies) and the system had to be restructured. The conversion to pay-as-you-go financing was inevitable; it became obvious that each active generation would have to provide for the inactive generations out of the current national income. In the wake of these events, the system was gradually opened to nearly all parts of German society.

Pensions at present are paid from three main sources:

(1) a compulsory general public system for employees, voluntary membership for the self-employed, and some special public systems;

(2) the pension schemes of private firms, which have grown most noticeably in recent years; and

(3) voluntary private life insurance, partly tax privileged.

The general public pension scheme is intended to be the main income source of aged persons, whereas private pensions and life insurance provide for greater security. For 1977, total benefits from the three sources amounted to about DM 134 billion (79.0 percent) from social insurance, DM 16 billion (10.0 percent) from the insurance of private firms, and DM 19 billion (11.0 percent) from private life insurance (Schmidt-Kaler 1979, p. 559). Other forms of benefits are also available to the elderly, such as welfare and housing assistance. Altogether it is estimated that total 1979 social transfer payments amounted to DM 425 billion, which is slightly more than 30.0 percent of GNP. Pensioners receive 38.4 percent of this, excluding health insurance payments (see Deutscher Bundesrat 1980).

The German public pension system includes several different subsystems:

• a general system financed mostly by contributions and divided into systems for blue-collar, white-collar, and mine workers;

• special systems for government officials[2] and war victims financed entirely from general tax revenues, and for farmers financed primarily from that source; and

• an industrial injuries scheme financed by employers' contributions.

To some extent, beneficiaries, especially widows, can cumulate benefits between and within the different subsystems.

Most revenues for the general system come from contributions raised on a pay-as-you-go basis, but supplemented by a federal subsidy that has been relatively declining in recent years (from 23 percent of total revenues in the 1960s to about 14 percent in 1981).[3] The present contribution rate is 18.5 percent of gross wages up to a ceiling of DM 52,800 per year, in most instances shared equally between employers and employees. The ceiling is increased annually in accordance with average wage increases. By and large, individual benefits depend on contributions, providing pensions for disability, retirement, and surviving dependents. Pensioners' contributions to the public health insurance scheme are also paid from the social pension system.

In general, the retirement age is 65, but since 1972 an earlier option has been available (the "flexible retirement age" of 63 for men and 60 for women and for unemployed persons). An earnings test applies only to early retirement. Since 1957 pensions have been adjusted annually to growth of nominal income—which means pensions increase to reflect both inflation and real income growth. Pensions are determined by four factors:

(1) the relative income position during total working life of the insuree;
(2) the number of pensionable years (years for which contributions were paid as well as times for education, etc.);
(3) a general fixed increase in rate, usually of 1.5 percent, for every pensionable year (for miners, 2.0 percent); and
(4) a general basis of valuation, estimated as the mean of the average gross wages in the past three years before retirement (in 1981, e.g., DM 24,686).

Partly because of World War II and partly because of the shorter working lives of female employees, the average number of pensionable years in 1977 was thirty-eight for men and twenty-five for women—which translates into pension levels for an average relative income position of 47.0 percent and 37.5 percent, respectively, of the general basis of valuation. Because of growing insurance periods and higher female labor participation, these levels are increasing; in the long run they will exceed 60.0 percent for forty and more pensionable years.

In 1972 the benefit system was greatly liberalized, as self-employed people and spouses were allowed to join the system and to make contributions retroactively on very favorable terms for past years. In the same year the already mentioned flexible retirement age and a regulation which comes close to a minimum pension were introduced, and pensioners' contributions to social health insurance were taken over by the social pension system. Most of these changes bore the character of redistributive transfers to the new classes of beneficiaries.

Today's social security system covers nearly everyone, but the recent benefit changes will impose severe problems on the system in the future.

PAST, CURRENT, AND FUTURE FINANCIAL PROBLEMS

The growing financial stresses on the German social security system must be viewed in relation to the enormous increase in all forms of public social spending in Germany since the 1880s. Adding to existing programs is politically far easier than reducing or replacing them, so few programs are ever reexamined. The bias and momentum toward ever-increasing social spending continues unchecked. Because of this one-way road toward more and more, the ratio of total real transfers (including social insurance) to real GNP has doubled since 1950, whereas real public expenditures for goods and services in relation to real GNP, after remaining constant for a long period of time, have actually declined in recent years. Growing transfers, by themselves, are responsible for the rapid growth of the German public sector.

A major reason for the explosion of benefit payments in the retirement insurance program results from the benefit formula just discussed. In the short term, conditions were favorable. Unfortunately, the long-run impacts were far more burdensome than the short-term effects; for instance, the retroactive payments for past years brought an immediate influx of revenue and thereby led to short-run improvements, but long-term obligations present a very different picture, exceeding contributions three—to sixfold.

As a result of the dynamic of this system, despite continuous economic growth at nearly full employment and an increasing number of contributors, in the mid-1960s expenditures began to exceed revenues. To meet this short-term deficit, an increase of the contribution rate from 14 percent in 1967 to 18 percent in 1973 was necessary. Serious recession exposed the limits of the system and it nearly collapsed.

The 1974-1975 recession produced a serious decline in contributions. As it became obvious that the high unemployment rates of this period were structural rather than cyclical and that liquidity reserves had been severely depleted to finance current expenditures, politicians tried to reduce expenditures shortly after the 1976 federal elections, contrary to all election promises and for the first time in postwar Germany. New and important changes came in 1978. First, automatic pension adjustments were reduced for the period from 1979 to 1981. In 1979 pensions increased only 4.5 percent instead of the 7.0 percent called for by the former benefit schedule; similar reductions were made in 1980 and 1981. Beyond that, adjustments were deferred six months. In 1981 the contribution rate was increased from 18.0 to 18.5 percent, and beginning in 1983 individual pensioners will again be required to contribute to health insurance.

These major changes and the real economic growth in 1979 combined with a decline in unemployment to improve the system's financial condition. The last estimates of expenditures and revenues show that from 1980 to 1983 liquidity reserves will increase, but this improvement will occur only if no serious recession takes place. Since recent forecasts are rather pessimistic, with negative growth expected for 1981 a new collapse seems likely.

In 1980 the so-called "pensioners' mountain" of the mid—and late 1970s will have passed (see figure 1). From 1980 to 1990 the ratio of people aged 60 and over to people aged between 15 and 60 will remain relatively constant.[4] The government argues that, if the law is not changed and no serious recessions occur, no serious problems are ahead of us. But experience shows that the number of pensions paid tends to increase faster than the number of people who reach the normal retirement age, which will put new stresses on the system. Another source of pressure has already appeared in the form of a Federal Constitutional Court judgment that the present system violates the constitutional requirement of equal rights for men and women, thus forcing the federal parliament to restructure survivors' benefits. Better provision for widows is also intended—which is important but is likely to be very expensive, no matter what the politicians say. Whatever changes are proposed, the great task will be to avoid short-sighted solutions. A good rule would be to stay away from new expenditures without making compensating reductions elsewhere.

Table 1

Ratio of workers to retirees[a]

Year	Workers (millions)	Retirees (millions)	Ratio of workers to retirees
1975	24.5	10.2	2.40
1980	24.7	11.3	2.19
1985	25.2	11.7	2.15
1990	25.5	12.1	2.11
1995	24.9	12.6	1.98
2000	24.1	13.2	1.83
2005	23.3	14.0	1.66
2010	22.5	14.4	1.56
2015	21.4	14.5	1.48
2020	20.0	14.6	1.37
2025	18.3	14.7	1.24
2030	16.7	14.9	1.12

Source: Petersen (1981b).

[a]Excluding public pensions for *Beamte*.

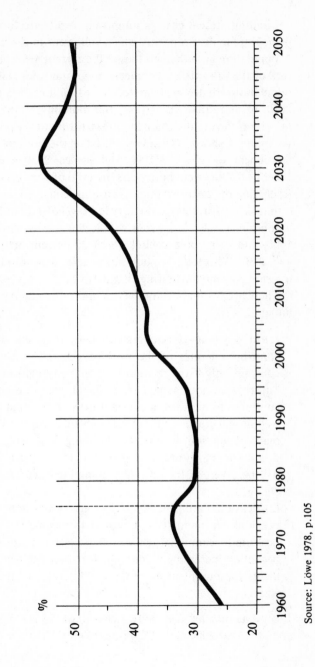

Figure 1

Dependency Ratio of Aged Persons in the Federal Republic of Germany
1960-2050

Source: Löwe 1978, p.105

Limiting present costs is important to prepare for dramatic demographic developments which will occur in the late 1990s. If population growth continues at the current net reproduction rate of 0.65 (a rate of 1.0 means a constant population), the population will decline from today's 61 million to 45 million in 2030, or more than 20 percent. But more important than this number is the rapidly changing age structure of the population. As figure 1 shows, Germany will be at the bottom of a new pensioners' mountain in 1990, and the year 2030 could see another peak. Between those years the ratio of workers to retirees (excluding the *Beamten* public pensions) could decline from an estimated 2.11 in 1990 to the very low level of 1.12 in 2030. The number of employed persons will decline slowly until the year 2000, and then could decline about 30 percent between 2000 and 2030. With today's pension formula, expenditures would increase enormously during that period.

There are two important defects in the German pension formula:

(1) In a pay-as-you-go system, pension levels as well as contribution rates of the working generation can be kept constant only if the relation between pensioners and contributors does not change. If, as in the past, the population continues to increase, a constant pension formula can work well; it will create no financial problems. But the West German population is already declining and will probably decline in the future, and problems in the pension system will be severe if the currently committed benefits stay unchanged.

(2) Pensions are linked to average *gross* wages. Since pensions are factually not subject to income tax[5] and it is possible to cumulate pensions from different sources, it is becoming increasingly common for total net pension payments to amount to more than 100 percent of the last *net* wage.

If we assume an average real growth of 3.5 percent in GNP up to the year 2000 and of 2.4 percent until 2030, the contribution rate will have to be increased from 18.5 percent today to 32.0 percent, presuming constant current net reproduction rate and pension levels. Lower economic growth would lead to an even higher increase. Naturally, these estimates are rather speculative. But at the moment, higher future growth rates are not very likely; there are also no signs of a substantial change in generative behavior which would be necessary to improve the future ratio of workers to retirees. It is obvious that, to secure the above presumed growth rates, a lot of technological progress and rapid structural changes would be needed, combined with increasing incentives for additional work. The problem here, as in other dimensions of social security, lies in what these rate increases will do to work incentives.

EFFECTS ON THE OVERALL ECONOMY

A great deal has been written about the allocative effects of social security on the overall economy—effects on both saving and employment. We have touched on the potentially harmful long-term employment effects of high and rising tax and contribution rates. Before we elaborate on these long-term effects, however, let us consider some principal questions and their relevance to the German case.

In particular, two hypotheses are controversially discussed: (1) negative impacts of private saving behavior because social security contributions are viewed as an alternative to saving, and (2) overall impacts that might result from the two financing principles of either reserve funding or pay-as-you-go.

An alternative to saving

People save for a variety of reasons, so it is rather difficult to distinguish between saving for retirement and for other purposes. Consequently, in measuring the effects of social security on personal saving, any number of substitution effects might be found. Nevertheless, some studies seem to prove a negative impact of social security on private saving behavior. For Germany, an empirical test of that question is impossible, since all time series available are already influenced by a long-lasting social retirement system. But apart from this, we have some doubts that saving behavior changed when the system was introduced in 1889. Before then, the majority of people covered by the new retirement system was not able to save at all.

The question remains, however, whether saving rates would have been higher during the last century without a public retirement system. In cross-country analyses where different levels of social security are compared with the connecting saving rates, some empirical studies show a negative correlation. But Germany today, for instance, has about the highest social security contribution rates of any developed country (in 1981 roughly 34 percent of gross wages for retirement, health, and unemployment insurance), while German saving rates also are among the highest. It seems that tax and subsidy provisions, national attitudes, institutional regulations, etc., are *more* important factors in influencing saving behavior than the question of a public versus a private pension system. And since incomes from property and wealth do not affect the level of public retirement pensions at all, this is another reason why social retirement insurance does not necessarily have a negative impact on personal saving.

Reserve funding or pay-as-you-go

The second question seems to be rather unimportant for Germany, because there is, in fact, no choice. As discussed above, after World War II Germany had to switch over to pay-as-you-go, and today a contribution rate of 18.5 percent is not even high enough to meet all current expenditures.

Germany is in a phase of decreasing population and therefore a declining number of insurees, which means—reserve funding presumed—that to finance the current pensions either reserves must be used or contributions must be increased. Switching over from pay-as-you-go to reserve funding would mean a sharp increase in contribution rates if reserve funds are to be built.[6] But a heavy impact on private saving is then likely, apart from possible disincentive effects which could impair future growth potential. Finally, in terms of real goods, each working generation pays taxes and contributions to support retired generations. (For a detailed discussion, see especially Mackenroth 1957, pp. 43-74.)

The marginal burden of taxes and contributions

Future economic growth will determine to what extent contributions will have to be increased and/or benefits reduced. On the other hand, it is often argued that accumulating a reserve fund would help to promote growth in order to overcome the current phase of relative stagnation; but the evidence on this is not encouraging. For instance, a closer look at the capital investment policies of German life insurance companies reveals a safety-first attitude, partly due to legal requirements. Private insurance systems seem to prefer a risk-averse portfolio. It is an illusion, therefore, to expect private insurance companies to provide the venture capital for rapid growth, and it would be far more questionable if public systems did it.

There are more promising opportunities to promote growth policies and to reduce public concern about social security— particularly, in the latter case, with regard to regulations affecting the labor market.

Effects of social security on employment are both short term and long term. The earnings test has an important short-term impact. Before 1972 the retirement age was 65 for both men and women and there was no earnings test; pensioners received their full pension entitlement no matter how much they earned. In 1972 options for earlier retirement were introduced, and at that time some restrictions were applied to the flexible retirement age of 63 and to early retirement at age 60. At present, monthly wages of DM 1,320 or DM 550, respectively, are allowed without loss of benefits.

Since these options for earlier retirement were offered without reducing benefits, there were strong incentives to retire early. The only disincentive, in fact, was the earnings test, which affected many people not at all. These generous options for early retirement have reduced the labor force and have strained revenues, forcing increased contributions. When these regulations were introduced, unemployment among the elderly was a serious concern; but disincentives to employment in the long run are hurting the overall economy and are placing short-term stresses on the social security system.

Very important—in both short and long term—is the impact on employment incentives for the normal working population of high and rising tax and contribution rates. To understand the extent of this problem, one must consider the total burden of current taxes and contributions. Figure 2 illustrates with figures from the wage scale for public employees (*Angestellte*). In the lowest wage group, an unmarried employee's marginal tax rate is 39.0 percent, including social insurance contributions; the marginal rate rises to 58.7 percent for a middle wage group, and after that it declines because the contribution ceiling for compulsory health insurance is reached. The rate increases in succeeding wage groups until, in the third but last group, the limits for retirement and unemployment are reached. After that, marginal rates increase only because of progression in the income tax.

The following percentages are marginal tax and contribution rates for a middle wage group (see Petersen 1981*a*):

(1) wage tax   41.7 percent
(2) employee contribution   17.0 percent
(3) church tax   3.8 percent
(4) indirect taxes   7.0 percent

The marginal burden thus reaches its maximum at about 70 percent excluding employers' contributions, or more than 80 percent including them. Unless there are substantial changes in tax and social law during the 1990s,[7] these marginal burdens will increase sharply if contribution rates alone are increased to hold today's pension levels to the current pension formula. Taking inflation into account, considering that the German tax

Figure 2
Marginal Tax Rates for Public Employees
(Angestellte) 1979

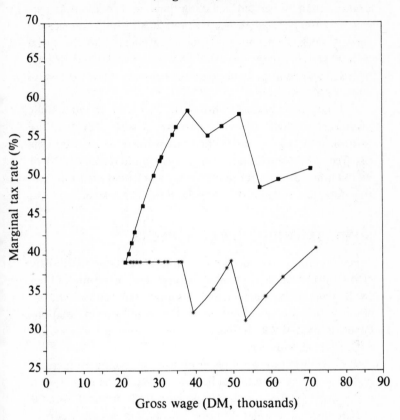

Code: ■ unmarried employees *married employees.

Source: Petersen 1981a.

system is not indexed for inflation, a real decline in the employees' net after-tax income is likely.

Compared to other Western countries, the Federal Republic of Germany has already reached a threshold of marginal burdens, especially for middle-income groups. Passing this threshold by further increases in marginal rates (e.g., to about 76 percent in the year 2000 excluding employers' contributions or to more than 90 percent including them, and to about 85 percent and 100 percent, respectively, in 2030) would constitute a serious work disincentive. A mass movement into the social welfare system cannot be ruled out, because social welfare payments are sometimes higher than the net incomes of workers in comparable situations.

As marginal burdens continue to increase, so will public awareness of them. Negative impacts on work incentives are possible if not likely, and we fear a growing movement into the tax-free and contribution-free underground economy. This would limit revenues more than ever, and would probably lead to a complete collapse of the social insurance system.

SOME DISTRIBUTIONAL ASPECTS

Few attempts have been made to analyze the redistributive effects of the German social retirement system within and between generations. Such an analysis must consider both the tax and benefit system, and not simply the benefit side in isolation. Given limited work in the area, the following remarks are necessarily speculative.

Redistribution between generations is becoming an increasingly important issue in public debate. While the mass media and special interest groups (especially trade unions) are still looking for additional "improvements" in social security, economists have begun to reflect on future problems, the first concerning the pension formula itself. Net pensions tend to increase more than net wages, since pensions are linked to average gross wages and are not taxed. Combined with rising contribution rates, this leads to a relative reduction of contributors' disposable income in favor of pensioners, a trend intensified by the growth of supplementary pensions and of income for pensioners from property which is taxed at low rates or not at all.

Regarding redistribution among those at work, following are some major variations in the way different workers are treated:

• Workers are taxed differently on their contributions. Because of varying tax exemptions (granted whether or not contributions are actually paid) depending on invididual income, marital status, and number of children, contributions are partly taxed and partly untaxed. Government officials, for example, get the same tax exemptions as other employees even though they pay no contributions for retirement security, and those exemptions reduce their taxable income.

• While contribution rates at any given time are unrelated to the number of children in a family at that moment, contribution rates, as noted above, depend very much on the relation between pensioners and contributors. The future number of contributors (and eventually, of pensioners) depends on the current number of children born, so future contribution rates are affected by current numbers of children. But families with children are not fully compensated for their part in sustaining the "generation treaty." Rather, they seem to be punished. As Schmidt-Kaler (1980, p. 70) has written, "The costs of children are largely privately borne, whereas the returns of children are socialized." Zeppernick (1979, p. 298) calls this effects "a completely underestimated redistribution mechanism between families with children and families without children." Some contributors attribute the decline in the fertility rate to this factor, at least in part.

• Parts of the German population are not included in the social retirement insurance scheme, notably the self-employed (who can become voluntary members) and government officials. Direct future burdens resulting from a declining population will therefore be borne only by compulsory members. Government officials will escape increasing contribution rates because their pensions are financed out of general tax revenues.

- A declining yet considerable share of total expenditures is financed by general revenue transfers. The redistributive effect of this reflects the redistributive effect of the whole tax system. The assumption seems to be correct that most redistribution measures only shift the burden within middle-income groups.

Redistribution within retired generations is linked to income distribution during their active years, but weakly. Because of World War II and other events, many of today's retired people receive low pensions due to their short qualifying periods. The introduction of a minimum pension in 1972 has reduced this problem, but widows in particular, who can claim 60 percent of their husbands' pensions, often have to live below the subsistence level. Of course, they have a claim on social welfare payments, but their children—if they can—have to reimburse what they receive. The "centenary" reform of 1984 will focus on this problem; an increase to 70 or 75 percent of the insurees' pension titles is currently under discussion.

Another problem concerns the cumulation of pension benefits from different sources, especially those for public employees (*Angelstellte*). The latter are compulsory members of the general social system and of an additional pension system which is supposed to raise their pensions to roughly 75 percent of their last gross wages. Since the pensions of public employees, financed by contributions, are untaxed, their net pensions often far exceed 100 percent of their last net wages. This is true for public employees at the upper end of the income scale as well as for singles, because both are subject to high marginal tax rates during their working lives. The effect is reinforced by the fact that additional incomes (e.g., from property and wealth) often are not reported and, if reported, are taxed at lower rates because of the high tax exemptions for pensions.

Summarizing, some redistributive elements within the social retirement system tend to favor the retirees with lower pensions. But the current tax regulations leading to factually untaxed pensions especially favor the well-to-do. It is difficult, therefore, to appraise the net redistributive effects of this uncoordinated tax and transfer system for the aged.

THE CURRENT POLITICAL CLIMATE

Despite criticism, there is broad public support for a social insurance system in Germany. That support is so strong, in fact, that a well-timed, substantial reform will be difficult to implement. This may be why the political parties offer such relatively short-sighted solutions which do not address broader systemic problems, in particular those caused by demographic changes. On the contrary, to overcome relatively short-term labor market problems, solutions are considered which will only intensify future problems. This is particularly true of attempts to improve the labor market by enlarging the flexible retirement age and by further shortening the work week (more rapidly than productivity increases will allow)—proposals which will probably come to be regarded as inviolable rights and entitlements and which therefore will become irreversible. If so, all measures together will impair Germany's future growth potential.

Current official reports discuss three measures in particular:

(1) reestablishing an individual pensioner's contribution to social health insurance;
(2) changing the pension formula to adjust pensions at a percentage of net wages (after income tax and social security contributions); and
(3) changing the basis for employers' contributions from individual wages to total value-added of a firm (a so-called "machine tax").

Some politicians believe that the first measure alone would solve future problems. Up to now, contributions for social pension insurance also pay for pensioners' health insurance. But before individual contributions to health insurance are introduced, pension benefits will be raised by the same amount; this increase then will be reduced gradually to 50 percent of health contributions. With regard to restraining expenditures, in fact, this measure is very weak and its redistributive effects are uncertain. The annual adjustment according to a percentage of net wages will reduce further pension increases but will leave the system's cumulative effects unchanged. The third measure (machine tax) is "revenue neutral."[8]

Other proposals have also been made by individual scholars and by commissions. Switching to reserve funding is frequently proposed—but this train, as noted above, has already left the station. Accelerated immigration of foreign manpower is also proposed to compensate for the increased German burden of aged persons, a burden which can be lessened only if the labor force is doubled between now and 2030. Since other developed countries face similar problems, it would be necessary to encourage the immigration of skilled workers from newly developing countries, thus causing a brain drain from those countries and sacrificing their current development strategies. Beyond that, several proposals concern the fact that contribution and benefit formulas do not take account of the demographic reproduction aspect.

The idea of increasing the general retirement age to 70, for instance, has not been raised in Germany and is not likely to be. In fact, there is currently talk of further reductions of the retirement age to solve labor market problems. If increasing the retirement age is not seriously considered, the reason can be found in the extent to which the retirement age of 65—which was established before World War I—has come to be regarded as a right (*sozialer Besitzstand*) which may not be violated. The existing flexible retirement system, however, is already open for a longer working life than 65, but incentives for the choice to work longer are not very strong. Incentives can be improved easily, leaving to the individual the free choice to retire, whereas a compulsory later general retirement age might result in a higher share of pensions paid to the disabled.

CONCLUSIONS

With a threat of bankruptcy hanging over the entire system, prospects for the German social pension system are rather gloomy. It is true that financial problems are nothing new; in the past they were always overcome by reforms—mostly by increasing contributions. But apart from the new beginning after World War II, the current system is faced with unprecedented problems. This is especially true of the demographic changes.

Four major problems plague the current system:

(1) The present system is so complex that, when it is combined with the possibility of cumulating benefits from different systems, no one really knows the actual financial status of a pensioner's household in Germany. This lack of information favors tendencies to add new programs, never to cut back old ones.

(2) This lack of knowledge is further confused by an uncoordinated tax and transfer system. Some pensions—such as the scheme for government officials—are taxed, but most are not. Pensioners' net incomes thus tend to increase faster than those of employees.

(3) With benefits rising more rapidly than contributions, the financial capacity of the system is almost exhausted. In the past, requests for increased and liberalized benefits were often granted without actuarial adjustments in contributions and benefits. In 1972 the self-employed were allowed to join social insurance and to take out subsequent insurance on extremely favorable terms. The flexible retirement age was not accompanied by an actuarial discount of pensions. At the time these changes were made, the costs were hidden; the great burden is still to come.

(4) Finally, the contribution and benefit formulas were more or less designed for an increasing population; they are not flexible enough to cope with fluctuating demographic developments as well.

Most proposals currently being considered contain worth-while elements:

- Initiating individual payments by pensioners for their health insurance.
- Inserting demographic criteria into retirement insurance.
- Removing disincentives towards female employment and introducing special maternity allowances.

Other measures, too, should be implemented:

- Intensify coordination and integration of the different social insurance subsystems, integrating especially the government officials' (*Beamte*) pension scheme into the general system.
- Impose ordinary income taxation on pensions and other incomes of the elderly to correct the tendency of the present tax and transfer system to discriminate against working generations in favor of pensioners.
- Eliminate or restructure most "reforms" introduced during the last decade without an actuarial surcharge or discount; for instance, this would mean discounting benefits for people retiring earlier than 65 and increasing them for those retiring later.

Even with these and other reforms, doubts remain whether the present German pension system can survive. The most fundamental problem lies in a prevailing attitude in both political parties and bureaucracies that people are as poor, as uninformed, and as incapable of providing for themselves as they were when the country was much poorer in the last century. Therefore, this attitude concludes, the government has responsibility to do everything—and everyone has a right to an unlimited number of the resulting benefits.

Fundamental reform—which treats more than symptoms and goes to the roots—would restructure our social security system to increase reliance on individual responsibility. With such reform, compulsory social security would provide only basic protection, leaving further protection to individual choice. The reformed system could bring together diverse elements and be integrated into the current overall tax system, including a negative income tax and indexation for inflation. In fact, German social security is already moving in this direction, incorporating degrees of coverage through firms' pension programs, through individual life insurance, and through other forms of individual saving—partly tax privileged.

A long-term perspective is as badly needed as it is regrettably absent. Because of its long development, social security obviously cannot be reformed overnight; we must commit ourselves to a long, slow process. The size of the German population is almost certain to experience a substantial decline in the decades just ahead. For this reason, unless social security benefits are reduced substantially or taxes and contributions increased, the present system will probably collapse. Between these policy options, increasing taxes is not a viable alternative at this point because high and rising taxes will have seriously negative incentive effects. The other alternative is to reduce benefits.

Solutions must somehow be found to safeguard the so-called "generation treaty" without imposing a hopeless burden on either current or future working generations. Maintaining tax burdens within tolerable limits is particularly important to maintain future economic growth which will permit increases in real income—or, at least, prevent declines. The challenge is there. We are sure that a free society will be flexible enough to find answers to it.

10

A. LAWRENCE CHICKERING
JEAN-JACQUES ROSA

A Political Dilemma

The vulnerability of social security programs. A future funding
crisis. Demographic changes and the dependency ratio. Pension levels, payroll taxes, and program costs. Indexation.
Redistribution and the equity problems.

Public retirement programs test in a fundamental way the ability of the political process to make and sustain sensible public policy. The essential problem with these programs is that they occur over a vastly longer period than the relatively short time perspectives of most politicians. As a result, they are extremely vulnerable to politicians' temptation to vote short-term benefits, transferring the much longer term costs into the future—to their successors or to future taxpayers, some of them not yet even born.

All of the programs studied here except that of Japan have pay-as-you-go financing systems in which current workers pay taxes to support pensions for current retirees. When economies are growing, and especially when an expanding population brings a growing number of workers to pay increasing benefits, the systems can support steadily expanding benefits. When economic growth declines, however, or when changes in the age structure of the population reduce the number of workers paying to support benefits for each retiree, the "chain letter" aspect of pay-as-you-go systems can create serious problems. This is especially true if politicians continue to increase benefits, knowing that changes in the birthrate will only reduce the numbers of workers paying taxes *in the future*.

This is exactly the situation for each of the countries in this book with a pay-as-you-go system. Since these countries are facing dramatic population aging, the expected decline in number of workers paying into their programs for each retiree will cause a funding crisis for these programs sometime after the turn of the century.

Japan has a largely funded system and thus is not vulnerable as are the other countries to demographic deterioration. The Japanese system has nevertheless fallen victim to the short-term political perspective in another form. A funded system will only build future security if the fund is invested so that it will give positive returns, yielding future benefits. Unfortunately, Japanese politicians have been unable to avoid the temptation to invest their social security fund in below-market, negative-return (in real terms) public investments and thus are forcing future social security beneficiaries to subsidize current public investment projects. This policy, not surprisingly, is dissipating the program's capital fund; if continued, it seems likely that Japan will resort increasingly to pay-as-you-go financing to meet its pension obligations.

ECONOMICS, DEMOGRAPHICS, AND POLITICS

Beyond the broad problems and the common political dilemma, this study of eight industrial countries shows some substantial and interesting differences in countries and programs.

Although most nations, assuming the continuation of present trends, will have a future funding crisis after the end of this century, the components influencing that crisis—especially pension levels and the ratio of workers paying taxes to retirees receiving pensions—vary widely from country to country. Japan, for instance, had 8.8 workers in 1980 paying for pensions averaging 45 percent of last wages (the replacement rate) for each retiree. Italy, on the other hand, had an incredibly low 1.41 workers in 1980 supporting pensions up to 80 percent of last earnings for each private worker (the number is higher for government workers), and Italy has a very serious current problem.

Benefit levels

Pension levels for most countries in this study fall in the narrow range of 40 to 50 percent. But Sweden pays 60 percent; Switzerland, now reforming its system, is about to pay a similar percentage; and Italy, as noted, pays up to a staggering 80 percent for private workers and even more for public workers. It is thus not surprising that those countries have very high current or expected payroll tax rates—20.65 percent for Sweden, 24.2 percent for Italy, and well over 20 percent expected in Switzerland after the imminent reform. Moreover, Italy and Switzerland require transfers from general revenues on top of payroll tax revenues to finance their current benefits. The incentive effects of these tax rates may be understood by considering that Italy and Sweden have very large underground economies; substantial and growing fractions of their work forces operate outside the official economies in order to escape taxes. Since for both countries high social security taxes are a major part of this problem, it is clear why policymakers are reluctant to raise taxes any further—and also why, in so many countries, nerves are on edge in anticipation of large tax increases after the turn of the century. In this respect, Italy offers a window on the future since its current tax, supplemented by a transfer from general revenues, is almost exactly what some projections assume the U.S. rate eventually will have to be to maintain currently legislated benefits.

If the present reveals serious problems for certain of these retirement systems, the future, as we have seen, is even bleaker in most countries. Here demographic trends are to blame, seriously reducing the numbers of workers paying to support retirees in the pay-as-you-go systems. Again, the numbers vary significantly between countries. Sweden has a relatively high ratio of workers to pensioners today (6.84 in 1980), and despite declining birthrates, will continue to have a relatively high ratio into the next century—3.44 in 2020. Sweden's funding problem comes, rather, from its very high benefit levels which, including medical benefits, amount to just under 15 percent of gross national product (GNP). This compares with GNP shares of 10 to 12 percent for most countries in this study and only 3.75 percent for Japan in 1978. Sweden's future ratio is high even in comparison to seven current rates, including those of Japan at 1.6 in 2025 (assuming Japan has a largely pay-as-you-go system then), Italy at 1.32 in 2000,[1] and West Germany at almost one worker (1.12, actually) for each retiree in 2030. In comparison with these figures, the policymakers' concerns pale in Great Britain and the United States, where declines are projected to 2 each in 2030 and 2035 respectively.

In considering these projections, it is important to recognize their limitations, particularly after the turn of the century, since they depend on estimates of future fertility and mortality rates. Most of the numbers above project current fertility and mortality rates into the future, and although for fertility the projections may be reasonable, there is good reason to believe that for mortality they are conservative, since continued health improvements are likely to increase future life expectancies. If so, the ratios given here are too optimistic: since the denominator will rise, the real ratios should be even lower than those above. In the case of Japan, in fact, Noriyuki Takayama based his projections on an assumed *increase* in fertility rates from the current level of 1.8 children per family to 2.1. If the current rate continues, of course, his projections will prove to be too optimistic.

However the ultimate numbers work out precisely, it seems clear that all of these programs (including Japan's if it goes to a pay-as-you-go system) face the unhappy choice either of continuing to increase taxes (payroll taxes or transfers from general revenues) or of reducing future pension levels. The latter option in the past has been extremely difficult to do. Nevertheless, unless they can find a way to reduce benefits, all the countries surveyed here face tax increases which, in most countries studied, could put payroll taxes in the new century at very high levels of more than 30 percent. The contributors to this book agree that such tax levels would cause great damage to the economies involved, some of which are already reeling under the heavy weight of taxation.

Japan's situation, again, is special because its 10 percent current tax rate is not especially high; with a reasonable return to its capital fund, it could maintain its funded system—including that actuarially sound tax rate—with a continued 20 percent transfer from general revenues. It is interesting that Japan's problem of dissipating its fund with below-market, negative-return investments is also evident in Sweden, which mandates accumulation of a large capital fund as part of its pay-as-you-go supplementary retirement system. The experience of these two countries—in which politicians are regulating investment of public funds in losing ventures, in effect—reveals the severe practical and political problems in trying to accumulate a capital fund to accommodate and soften future funding problems. Although such accumulations are frequently recommended by students of the long-term financing problem, the Japanese and Swedish experiences offer powerful evidence that this option may only invite squandering public capital funds in wasteful, low-yield public investments. Their experience should give pause to anyone proposing similar accumulations elsewhere.

If increasing payroll taxes is not the solution, what do these case histories indicate about political strategies for reducing pension levels? Unfortunately, the record here is extremely spotty. In the case of short-term funding crunches, West Germany was able to reduce benefits where economic necessity forced politicians to reverse long-term political promises to the contrary. Similarly, the United States in 1977 reformed and reduced its indexation formula, which double-indexed benefits to inflation—but only after several years during which the grossly overindexed formula was threatening to bankrupt the system. By the time the mistake was corrected, the replacement rate had risen from 31 to 45 percent, increasing benefits far more than wages during the same period and forcing tax increases in 1977 which were the largest in U.S. history.

If politicians have had trouble reducing benefits, even in the face of short-term bankruptcy, they have shown enormous reluctance ot consider solutions to the long-term funding problems which afflict all of these systems. The options, of course, are simple to identify: increase the retirement age, reduce the indexation formula, reduce current benefit levels—any or all of these things either in the present or in the future. The political problem, again, exists in asking politicians to impose *current* costs on large constituencies in order to solve *future* problems. The sooner reforms are undertaken, the easier it will be for all these systems to move across the demographic barrier; the longer they wait, the heavier the burden must be, both economically and politically.

In the United States and Japan, increasing the retirement age has seemed politically to be one of the most promising ways of reducing future benefits in terms of current value. In fact, raising the retirement age in the United States has been the *only* long-term solution which many politicians have been able to discuss openly. The reason for the appeal of this reform may be that it allows maintenance of annual benefits during pensionable years. This approach also makes substantive sense, since later entrances into the work force are shortening the working lives of program beneficiaries while lengthened life expectancies are increasing retirement periods. Establishing a higher retirement age also fits with the fact that jobs in postindustrial society on average are less strenuous than they were a generation ago. Increasing the retirement age, however, is not a serious possibility everywhere; Jüttemeier and Petersen write that in West Germany the social security system is assumed to be contractually bound to current retirement ages, so there is no discussion of increasing them as a way to reduce benefits and control program costs. And in France the government is currently contemplating the possibility of *reducing* the retirement age.

The indexation formula

In all countries, both fairness and politics require the institution of changes in benefit formulas to take effect *in the future* to avoid upsetting long-standing expectations either of current pensioners or of those soon to retire. Moderate changes in indexation formulas, however, may be possible to enact where efforts are made to encourage bipartisan sponsorship, and where there is broad public education and recognition that changes are unavoidable.

Apart from the political problems of reducing benefits, one major substantive question is whether indexation formulas should merely protect pensioners from the ravages of inflation, or whether they should go further and allow *increases* in real benefit levels as economies experience real growth. Should indexation, in other words, protect only *absolute* pension levels, or should it also protect pension levels *relative to* rising wage levels? Countries such as West Germany explicitly index to inflation plus real wage growth. Italy indexes with different formulas for different retirement programs, but the cumulative effect is to maintain pension increases 10 to 20 percent above the real inflation rate. Japan formally indexes only to inflation, but through legislation has increased real pension levels with economic growth. Switzerland indexes to inflation and 50 percent of real income growth; Britain, only to inflation; and France has no formal indexation at all, giving increases by explicit legislation. While the tendency in most countries has been to index for more than prices, it is not clear that this practice can continue in the difficult funding years ahead.

The question of the indexation formula also has important political implications, which go to the heart of the "implicit contract" underlying all pay-as-you-go social security systems. This contract creates implicit future obligations to pay pensions for workers who pay current taxes into the system. In fact, political support for the system—including especially the willingness of current workers to continue paying taxes that give them no formal legal claim to benefits—depends absolutely on perceptions of the strength of the implicit contract. Here, the anticipated future return on workers' "investment"— strongly influenced by the indexation formula, among other things—plays a critical role in shaping current perceptions of the contract. In this sense, of course, the long-term problem has important *present* consequences, particularly in the face of

dramatic declines in the expected return for younger generations now paying in. In a number of countries these returns
may actually become negative for some workers, and this prospect may fundamentally threaten the integrity of the implicit
contract and political support for it. These present consequences cause an immediate political problem, as voters factor
expectations of the future into their present behavior. The
crisis of social security should thus become an immediate
concern to officeholders. The political problem is *now*, and
politicians would do well to understand voters' intense current
interest in it.

In every case, it is essential that political support be ensured
by an explicit social contract which guarantees that current taxpayers will receive at least a reasonable market return on their
tax investment in the future. It is important that no one be
encouraged to think he would be better off diverting his payroll
taxes into alternative instruments.

The basic conceptual problem in almost all public retirement
programs is that they attempt to serve two very different purposes. As Rosen points out in relation to the United States, all
of these systems—even Japan's, which is largely funded—
attempt to combine insurance systems of earned entitlements
with a transfer element, allowing people to get back something
in proportion to what they pay in and transferring funds within
and between generations. In fact, the *mythology* of earned
entitlements in a pay-as-you-go setting has had the political
effect of largely insulating these transfer elements from the discipline imposed on the general revenue budget: since taxpayers
are encouraged to believe their payroll taxes are equivalent to
putting money in the bank, they have reason to acquiesce to
ongoing payroll tax increases to a much greater extent than to
increases in the general taxes they pay, which bear no relation
to perceived future benefits.

In response to this problem of conflicting purposes, most
students of social security recommend gradual separation of
the welfare (transfer) function from the earned entitlements
(insurance) function. In such a separation, basic minimum pen-

sions would be delimited and isolated from the rest, and should be financed by a payroll tax. And the transfer elements should gradually be transferred to the general revenue budget where they would have to compete with other priorities of public funding. Funded from general revenues, the transfers would thus come under fiscal discipline that has rarely been evident under current social security programs.

Moderating future benefit increases will increase the role that must be played by the private market in providing future income security for the elderly. This effect will have the added benefit of mitigating the problem of declining saving and investment rates in most industrial countries. Beyond that, however, the current program in Great Britain offers a model for encouraging competition and substitutability between programs by allowing pensioners to opt out of the supplementary public pension program in favor of approved private programs. The attractiveness of this option is indicated by the large percentage of those eligible to opt out who do so (90 percent).

Despite the appeal in this option, however, the problems in converting to increased flexibility are substantial. Since the first political and moral requirement of any proposed change must be to maintain the integrity of current obligations, opportunities are limited for people to opt out of current pay-as-you-go systems in favor of private *funded* systems. Somehow, the money must be found to finance current obligations, and the very reasons why pay-as-you-go systems are so attractive in program start-up phases make conversion to funding enormously difficult: at start-up, relatively large benefits can be paid to relatively few retirees, using low taxes from large numbers of taxpayers. This initial "free ride" means that later conversion to funding will require taxpayers to pay *twice*—once to support the current pay-as-you-go structure, and a second time to accumulate their own funded pensions. Given large constraints operating on public budgets everywhere today, this option is very difficult to imagine in practical terms.

Equity problems

Every system has its own equity problems, and little point would be served in recalling all of them here. There are two problems, however, that appear in all systems, and they are sufficiently serious to require attention in the near future.

The first concerns the long-term funding problem and the implicit contract. In the past, when economies were growing rapidly and populations were expanding, funding for pay-as-you-go systems seemed abundant, and it appeared both reasonable and fair to ask younger, richer generations to help support older, poorer ones. In fact, of course, such help had been operating in all societies in the form of private obligations. The enactment of public social security programs had the effect of socializing private obligations so that children now support their parents by sending money through public retirement programs. It is not our purpose here to judge the value or implications of substituting public for private obligations, although those implications are socially and psychologically enormous. Whatever judgment one chooses to make, the current long-term funding problems in social security are forcing policy-makers to reexamine these intergenerational social transfers in relation to other public social obligations. The value of this rethinking is, of course, reinforced by some regressive redistribution in these intergenerational transfers, since not all of the elderly are poor and some among the young are quite poor. The extent of the problem is highlighted in the case of Sweden, as Ingemar Ståhl makes clear, in its demonstration of the extremes to which a system can go in intergenerational redistribution.

Within generations, the progressivity of redistribution is much more in doubt. Social security programs often do not, in fact, make the rich give to the poor as is commonly assumed. Rather, the poor frequently give to the rich: on the one hand, lifetime contributions are roughly proportional to lifetime income, but pension levels are based on the best year's or the last year's earnings, and this combination favors those with steep career-earnings curves. Also, those who start work earlier give to the latecomers who are often better educated and earn more; those who die younger (who have lower incomes) give to those who live longer (with higher incomes); and bachelors give to women, who work a shorter period, retire earlier, and live longer. Moreover, the self-employed and civil servants often benefit from reduced contributions, and civil servants can often retire earlier.

The second broad equity problem, as Rosen points out, concerns the fact that many programs base calculations of costs and benefits on different accounting units. While taxes are paid on an individual basis, benefits are paid on a family basis, and this system of favoring women in their roles as spouses is causing great strains as it disadvantages women in their individual roles as taxpayers' beneficiaries. Guaranteed pension benefits as spouses, working wives in effect get no benefit for their payroll taxes paid as workers. As the role of women has changed and the labor force participation of women increased, the spouse benefit has come under increasing criticism. The unfairness is not, of course, to women *per se*, only to working women vis-à-vis nonworking spouses.

MANAGING THE TRANSITION

The most difficult step in reform will be designing a reasonable and politically acceptable transition between present systems—and their entitlement structures, which are difficult to meet—and new, reformed ones. In point of fact, what we have referred to as the "long-term funding problem" is not long term at all. The real problem is to finance the retirement of the postwar baby boom generation with taxes paid by a work force made smaller by the decline in birthrates. During this difficult period, many of the problems discussed in this book may be acute—including adverse impacts on savings, adverse incentive effects, and so on.

The more immediate dilemma, however, is to find a way to encourage policymakers and the public to take these issues

Table 1

Comparison of Basic Social Security Rates

Nation	Earn-ings test	Tax rate			Gene-ral reve-nue (%)	Percent of GNP		Replacement rate	
		Basic (%)	Supple-mental (%)	Ceil-ing[a]		Basic (%)	Supple-mental (%)	Basic (%)	Supple-mental (%)
Sweden	Yes	8.4	12.25	—	—	6.2[b]	3.3[b]	60.0 (combined)	
Japan	Yes	10.6 (m) 8.9 (f)	—[c] —[c]	$22.0M	20	3.76	—	45.0[d] (combined) 42.0/100.0[d]	
Germany	Yes	18.5	—	$22.0M	14	11.2	—	47.0 (m) 37.5 (f)	—
France	No	12.9	—	$10.5M	—	7.65	—	41.9	
Switzer-land	No	8.4	6.4	—[e]	16	5.8	4.1	150/50[e,i] (combined)	
Great Britain	Yes	20.45[f]	—	$16.0M	15	5.5 [g]	—	23.0	25.0
United States	Yes	12.26	—	$29.7M	—	12.8	—	45.0	—
Italy	Yes	24.2	—	—	13	12.0	—	30.0/80.0[h]	—

Key: M = thousand; (m) = male; (f) = female.

[a]Dollar value based on late currency prices at New York and San Francisco banks on 1 July 1981.

[b]Medical portion of Swedish social security is 5% of GNP.

[c]Japan's tax rate includes both basic and supplemental insurance.

[d]Average replacement rate in Japan is 45%. Japan's richest pensioners receive 42%; the poorest receive more than 100%.

[e]In Switzerland, the supplementary program is undergoing revision, which is expected to levy taxes of about 15% on incomes between $8.2M and $24.6M per year. In the basic program, there will continue to be no ceiling.

[f]The British tax rate is 7% less for those who choose to contract out of the government system.

[g]Private retirement insurance on those who contract out equals another 5% of GNP.

[h]Replacement rate in Italy ranges from 30% up to 80%.

[i]For couples with incomes between $3.6M and $21.8M.

seriously and act on them. As we have said, while politicians may think and hope that these problems are limited to the distant future and can certainly be solved by somebody else, those future problems have very definite *present* implications and consequences for younger generations of voter taxpayers. Since people routinely factor judgments of the future into their present decisions and actions, smart politicians would do well to consider the severe political dangers that go with continued pretenses as benign ignorance. The lessons in this book offer the basis for an important, serious debate on this issue. Unfortunately, the debate has yet to begin.

NOTES

3. Richard Hemming and John A. Kay : "Great Britain"

1. This joint contribution rate, along with all those referred to later in this chapter, include small contributions to the National Health Service and the Redundancy Fund amounting to no more than 1.2 percent.

2. There are two sources of cost savings. The first comes from the progressive reduction in the contracting out rebate to 4.5 percent over the first thirty years of the scheme. The second comes from a change in the treatment of married women. Prior to the introduction of SERPS, married women could opt to pay a reduced contribution rate and would receive no pension. This option is to be phased out, implying an increase in the tax base and a reduction in the contribution rate.

3. See Creedy 1980 for some provisional estimates of the difference between average lifetime earnings and the average of the best twenty years' earnings.

4. On these views, see Rosen 1977, and Leimer and Lesnoy 1980.

4. Onorato Castellino : "Italy"

1. The most up-to-date survey of all existing schemes may be found in an annex to Italy 1979a.

2. The number of workers insured under the "general" scheme (believe it or not) is unknown and may only be guessed, even by managers of the fund. The sudden increase between 1960 and 1965 is only due to the discontinuity of the series (of guesses). Schemes for the self-employed did not exist before 1955; they were established in 1957 for farmers, in 1959 for craftsmen, and in 1966 for tradesmen. The yearly contribution applies to craftsmen and tradesmen; for farmers, it was and is even smaller.

3. Since the social security deficit is paid by the treasury, its immediate impact is felt by the floating debt (money creation and treasury bills issue) which may or may not be funded at a later time, depending on overall public debt policy.

4. Figures in table 5 are roughly but not strictly comparable because of a discontinuity between 1970 and 1971 due to the adoption of a new system of national accounts. After 1977 separate figures for families and firms are not available. OASDI deficit covers the "general" scheme, the three main schemes for the self-employed, and welfare pensions.

5. The exact figure for 1980 is not yet available, but the 1971-1980 averages may be assumed to be the same as for 1971-1979.

6. Public enterprises, insofar as they produce salable goods and services, are not included in general government but in the firms' sector.

7. According to a recent sample (Banca d'Italia 1979), persons in no professional category (who largely, although not exactly, correspond to pensioners) have an *average* rate of saving of about half the figure emerging from the whole sample. The *marginal* rate of saving may, of course, be assumed to be higher than the average one.

8. The government share in the 1970s is actually negative in the United States as well as in Italy, but remains positive in the other countries.

9. In Italy, this destruction was particularly strong in 1973, 1974, 1976, 1979, when it amounted to 2.6, 6.1, 3.68, and 2.87 percent of GNP. The 1980 figure is also likely to be very high.

10. See Shoup 1969, pp. 412-13, and the papers by Samuelson and Mishan quoted there; also Brittain 1972, pp. 238-39. For Italy, see Valiani 1969, pp. 168-69.

5. Noriyuki Takayama : "Japan"

1. The seven programs are for employees of private enterprises with no less than five insured members, the central government, local governments, public corporations, private schools, institutions of agriculture, forestry, and fishery, and for seamen. The remaining one for others (mainly for self-employed people) imposes a flat-rate contribution and pays a flat-rate benefit. A more detailed explanation of the public pension systems in Japan, written in English, is given in Japan 1977, pp. 81-96.

2. Generally speaking, the KNH offers no benefits to men who have retired before age 60, whether mandated or not, unless special factors such as disability entitle them to pensions at a younger age.

3. The ceiling on which the payroll tax is levied is high, since it covers no more than 5 percent contributors and has been raised at least every five years. Thus, with its removal, revenues would not be that much increased.

4. The contribution rate t in case (1) is given by:
$$t = 0.6 \, [(1+r)^{15}-1] \, / \, [(1+r)^{15} \, (1+r)^{45}-1]$$
where r ($\neq 0$) is the real annual rate of return on investment.

5. The best survey is given by Gultekin and Logue 1979, upon whose work my summary in this chapter is principally based.

6. Pay-as-you-go financing in public pensions means that the government must engage in "deficit finance," as pointed out in Buiter and Tobin 1979, p. 54.

7. Socializing private transfers from children to their parents could increase private savings. In Japan, however, this is unlikely to occur, because children in low-income families would then increase their own consumption rather than their savings.

8. An intellectual survey of the effects of the work test is given in Rosen 1977, pp. 100-103.

9. We can easily conjecture that this incidence is derived from applying the Coase Theorem.

10. Principal assumptions in the estimated wealth value are as follows: (a) both the employee and the employer contributions are attributed to the employee; (b) the cohort pays an average tax per member in each year; (c) the relevant annual rate of interest and the discount rate are 6.5 percent in nominal terms; (d) the cohort contributed continuously for twenty-eight years.

11. The wealth difference between them will widen with the adjusted age difference.

12. The intergenerational transfer can involve a long-term inter-family transfer between different numbers of children. To offset this transfer might require the system to tax more heavily those people with no children or only one child than those with more children.

13. Taxing pension benefits with no particular deductions would increase general revenues.

14. This concern is twofold: to defend the young poor from paying high-rate regressive taxes in supporting their poor parents or relatives, and to repay an obligation of younger generations who benefit from the economic growth initiated with the savings or sacrifices of older generations.

15. Cost differences between mandatory and voluntary private pensions are given in Diamond 1977, p. 296. Another factor leading to a higher premium in voluntary private pensions is adverse selections, which can be avoided by mandating. See Feldstein 1977, p. 19.

16. Compulsory pensions as insurance can be financed on a pay-as-you-go basis if the growth rate of total personal income exceeds the rate of return on capital investment in the distant future. The economy in Japan now ceases to meet this requirement.

6. Ingemar Ståhl : "Sweden"

1. The latter figure still appears high in relation to other countries, but this figure includes only old-age pensioners and does not count survivor and disability pensions.

2. One major part of the SPP's operations prior to 1977 was to provide pensions for those between ages 65 and 67, the latter the retirement age of the ATP until 1977. Up to that year, the general practice for privately employed white-collar workers was to retire at age 65 and receive SPP pensions until age 67, the point at which the ATP began to pay. Some government employees' pension schemes are even more generous, with eligibility for pensions beginning at age 60 in some state corporations.

7. Martin C. Janssen and Heinz H. Müller : "Switzerland"

1. Data used in the text are from Switzerland, *Statistisches Jahrbuch der Schweiz*, various years, if not stated differently.

2. Conversions from Swiss francs (Sfr.) into dollars ($) are based on the average exchange rates of the respective years.

3. In 1978 per capita GNP was 30,000 Sfr. ($14,000).

4. The trust fund was originally intended to be a fully funded part of the basic component. It then became a reserve to cover the costs of increased life

expectancy, and later became a special reserve to cover future payments to foreign workers. Today it merely covers fluctuations between receipts and expenditures.

5. The hypothetical interest rate leading to equality of the present values of total payroll contributions and total benefits is called "internal rate of return."

6. Wealth stemming from the basic and supplementary components is, of course, not included in these figures. In 1976 the average (mean) wealth of retirees' households was 190,000 Sfr. ($76,000), while the median value was 68,000 Sfr. ($27,000). By comparison, the corresponding values for the whole adult population were 92,000 Sfr. ($37,000) and 28,000 Sfr. ($11,000). Figures are taken from Schweizer 1980, 1:79, 85.

7. For a definition of "normal phase," see below.

8. The point estimation of this rate of substitution is 0.9, but the confidence interval is rather large.

9. Additional welfare payments are made by the cantons and communities (financed out of their general revenues), as the minimum benefits of the basic program do not cover the officially declared subsistence level.

10. Compare, for example, Brunner 1967. Brunner has some interesting recommendations.

11. For identical contributions, a married couple draws 50 percent more than a single person.

12. Strictly speaking, the supplementary program is not (yet) mandatory.

13. Beyond the political reasons given above, this is also motivated by structural policy favoring small-scale industries and farmers.

14. This procedure would, of course, have allowed for upper and lower limits of benefits.

15. Milton Friedman's proposition to finance social security out of general revenues (cf. Friedman 1977, pp. 25-27) would probably not have been feasible on political grounds.

8. Sherwin Rosen : "United States"

1. Excellent sources of the history of the U.S. social security system are Witte 1962, Carlson 1962, and the reports of the Quadrennial Advisory Councils on Social Security. The latter, as well as *Trustee Reports on Social Security Trust Funds* and various issues of the *Social Security Bulletin*, are very good sources of program data.

2. For additional details, the reader is referred to Rosen 1977.

3. Martin Feldstein has pursued these issues at great length in publications too numerous to list. A good review of the issues and some of the technical studies is found in Boskin and Robinson 1980.

4. This point has been made by Kurz and Arvin 1979. Notice that insofar as the initial generations received windfall gains because they did not pay full taxes into the system, their real wealth was increased, enabling them to consume more than their own lifetime income—that is, net dissaving—and therefore reducing capital formation in that generation.

5. A useful review of the technical studies is found in Gustafson 1979.

6. The 1974 and 1979 reports by the Advisory Council on Social Security discuss these issues in great detail.

7. Useful technical descriptions of various indexing proposals are found in Campbell 1979, particularly in the papers by Hsiao and Kaplan.

9. Karl Heinz Jüttemeier and Hans-Georg Petersen : "West Germany"

1. The system had to be publicly organized because private insurance showed insufficient interest (perhaps due to the bad risk structures which would have pressed private insurance to adverse selection) and because wages were too low. The introduction of an employer's contribution and a state grant to the social retirement pension insurance could be compared to a state-forced wage increase.

2. In the Federal Republic of Germany there are two types of government officials: *Angestellte* and *Beamte*. Originally sovereign powers should only be exercised by *Beamte* and not by *Angestellte*. *Angestellte* belong to the general pension system and have to pay contributions, whereas *Beamte* belong to a special system without individual contributions. For *Angestellte*, an additional pension system exists to secure comparable benefit levels with those of the *Beamte*.

3. The federal grant originally was intended to finance the redistributive elements within the system, such as pensionable times without contributions (e.g., for education, employment), coinsurance of family members without contributions, and so on. Today this subsidiary aim is not reflected in the actual level of the federal grant.

4. The average retirement age is far less than the normal retirement age of 65, because many unemployed and women retire at age 60 and the majority of men at age 63. Additionally there are some political pressures to reduce retirement age, especially to solve labor market problems.

5. In principle, pensioners are covered by income tax, but various exemptions yield an untaxed pension of DM 32,500 per annum or, in the case of a married couple, about DM 55,600 per annum. For further details, see Petersen 1981*b*.

6. In the current situation in Germany, a total conversion to reserve funding would require increasing the contribution rate from 18.5 percent to 34.0 or 38.0 percent in the next five to ten years. See, e.g., Meinhold 1978.

7. At the moment, the German Federal Government faces severe financial problems which make future substantial tax reductions unlikely.

8. This proposal will only shift the burden within the business sector. But some people fear that with the "machine tax" a new redistributive instrument will be implemented which will put the future burden only on firms. Considering tax shifting, this possibility is an illusion.

10. A. Lawrence Chickering and Jean-Jacques Rosa : "A Political Dilemma"

1. This is the last year for which data are available in Italy, with further deadlines expected in the decades following.

REFERENCES

Banca d'Italia. 1979. "Reddito, risparmio et patrimonio immobiliare delle famiglie italiane nel 1978." *Bolletino* (July/September).

Bank of England. 1977. "The Personal Sector 1966-1975." *Bank of England Quarterly Bulletin*, March.

Barro, R. J. 1974. "Are Government Bonds Net Wealth?" *Journal of Political Economy*, July/October.

Belbin, R. M. 1978. "Retirement Age Policies and Options for Employment in Europe." In *Aging and Income*, ed. B. R. Herzog. New York: Human Science's Press.

Boettcher, Erik, ed. 1957. *Sozialpolitik und Sozialreform*. Tübingen, Federal Republic of Germany.

Boskin, Michael J., ed. 1977a. *The Crisis in Social Security*. Rev. ed. 1978. San Francisco, CA: Institute for Contemporary Studies.

_____. 1977b. "Social Security: The Alternatives before Us." In *The Crisis in Social Security*, ed. Michael J. Boskin. San Francisco, CA: Institute for Contemporary Studies.

_____. 1977c. "Social Security and Retirement Decisions." *Economic Inquiry* 15 (January).

_____, and Robinson, Marc. 1980. "Social Security and Private Saving: Analytical Issues, Econometric Evidence and Policy Implications." Study prepared for the U.S. Congress Joint Economic Committee (March). Washington, D.C.: U.S. Congress Joint Economic Committee.

Brittain, J. A. 1972. *The Payroll Tax for Social Security*. Washington, D.C.: The Brookings Institution.

Browning, E. K. 1979. "The Politics of Social Security Reform." In *Financing Social Security*, ed. C. D. Campbell. Washington, D.C.: American Enterprise Institute.

_____. 1975. "Why the Social Insurance Budget Is Too Large in a Democracy." *Economic Inquiry*, September.

Brunner, Andreas C. 1967. "Memorandum betreffend die Vorschläge für die Umstrukturierung der AHV." Zug, Switzerland: Landis & Gyr, AG.

Buiter, W. H., and Tobin, J. 1979. "Debt Neutrality: A Brief Review of Doctrine and Evidence." In *Social Security versus Private Saving*, ed. G. M. von Furstenberg. Cambridge, MA: Ballinger.

Bundesaufsichtsamt für das Versicherungswesen. 1979. *Geschäftsbericht 1978*. Berlin.

Campbell, Colin D. 1979. *Financing Social Security*. Washington, D.C.: American Enterprise Institute.

Caranza, C. 1980. "Gli effetti dello sviluppo economico e dell'inflazione sul risparmio: alcune considerazioni con riferimento all'esperienze italiana." *Note economiche* 1.

Carlson, Valdemar. 1962. *Economic Security in the United States*. New York: McGraw-Hill.

Collard, D. A.; Lecomber, J. R.; and Slater, M. D. E., eds. 1980. *The Limits to Redistribution*. London: John Wright and Sons.

Creedy, J. 1980. "The New Government Pension Scheme: A Simulation Analysis." *Oxford Bulletin of Economics and Statistics* 42.

Deutscher Bundesrat. 1980. *Sozialbericht 1980*. Drucksache 407/80. Bonn.

Diamond, P. 1977. "A Framework for Social Security Analysis." *Journal of Public Economics* 8 (December).

Dinkel, Reiner. 1980. "Alterssicherung bei stagnierender oder schrumpfender Bevölkerung als Zukunftsaufgabe der sozialen marktwirtschaft." Paper prepared for the Jahrstagung der Gesellschaft für Wirtschafts- und Sozialwissenschaftern in Nürnberg 1980. Munich.

Ermisch, J. 1980. *Paying the Piper: Demographic Changes and Pension Contributions*. London: Policy Studies Institute.

Feldstein, Martin. 1977. "Social Security." In *The Crisis in Social Security*, ed. Michael J. Boskin. San Francisco, CA: Institute for Contemporary Studies.

――――. 1974. "Social Security, Induced Retirement and Aggregate Capital Accumulation." *Journal of Political Economy* 82 (September/October).

Ferri, P., and Szegö, G. 1980. "La struttura del risparmio in un precesso di crisi." *Economia italiana*, October.

France. 1978. *Projection de la population totale de la France, 1975-2020*. Paris: Institut National de la Statistique et des Etudes Economiques (INSEE).

――――. 1980a. *Système de Retraite et Accumulation du Capital*. Rapport pour le Commissariat Général au Plan (Masson et Strauss-Kahn). Paris: Centre de Recherche Economique sur l'Epargne.

――――. 1980b. *Vieillir Demain*. Commissariat Général au Plan, report of the working group "Vieillir Demain" for preparation of the 7th Plan. Paris: Documentation Française.

Friedman, Milton. 1977. "Payroll Taxes, No; General Revenues, Yes." In *The Crisis in Social Security*, ed. Michael J. Boskin. San Francisco, CA: Institute for Contemporary Studies.

Geyer, Gotfried, and Genzke, Jürgen. 1980. "Die voraussichtliche finanzielle Entwicklung der gesetzlichen Rentenversicherung bis 1983." *Die Angestelltenversicherung* 27 (Berlin).

Giersch, Herbert, ed. 1981. *Towards Explaining Economic Growth*. Tübingen, Federal Republic of Germany.

Great Britain. 1974. *Better Pensions Fully Protected against Inflation: Proposals for a New Pension Scheme*. Cmd. 5713. London: Her Majesty's Stationery Office.

――――. 1981. *Occupational Pension Schemes 1979—Sixth Survey by the Government Actuary*. London: Her Majesty's Stationery Office.

_____. 1942. *Social Insurance and Allied Service*. Cmd. 6404. Known as the Beveridge Report. Reprinted 1969 (New York: Hagathon Press). London: Her Majesty's Stationery Office.

_____. 1979. *Social Trends*. London: Her Majesty's Stationery Office.

Gultekin, N. B., and Logue, D. E. 1979. "Social Security and Personal Saving: Survey and New Evidence." In *Social Security versus Private Saving*, ed. G. M. von Furstenberg. Cambridge, MA: Ballinger.

Gustafson, Thomas. 1979. "Labor Supply of the Elderly." In *Work, Income and Retirement of the Aged*. Technical Analysis Paper 18, Office of Income Security, Department of Health, Education, and Welfare. Washington, D.C.: HEW.

Hauser, Mark, and Meyer, Peter. 1980. *Die obligatorische Altersvorsorge in der Schweiz: Rentabilitätsüberlegungen und Einkommensumverteilungsaspekte*. Working paper. Zurich: Institute for Empirical Research in Economics, University of Zurich.

Hemming, Richard. 1978. "State Pensions and Personal Savings." *Scottish Journal of Political Economy* 25.

Herzog, B. R., ed. 1978. *Aging and Income*. New York: Human Science's Press.

Howard, D. H. 1978. "Personal Saving Behavior and the Rate of Inflation." *The Review of Economics and Statistics*, November.

Hsiao, William. 1979. "A Comparison of Rates of Return to Social Security Retirees under Wage and Price Indexing." In *Financing Social Security*, ed. Colin D. Campbell. Washington, D.C.: American Enterprise Institute.

Italy. 1978. *Bollettino mensile di statistica*. Rome: Istituto Centrale di Statistica.

_____. 1979a. *CNEL Report on Social Security Reforms* (January). Rome: Consiglio nazionale dell'economia e del lavoro.

_____. 1980. *Compendio statistico italiano 1980*. Rome: Istituto Centrale di Statistica.

_____. 1979b. *1980 Budget*. Rome: Istituto Nazionale della Previdenza Sociale.

Japan. 1977. *Health and Welfare Services in Japan*. Ministry of Health and Welfare. Tokyo: Toshida Finance & Social Security Law Institute.

_____. 1976. *Revised Financial Estimates of the KNH*. Ministry of Health and Welfare. Tokyo: Toshida Finance and Social Security Law Institute.

Jüttemeier, Karl Heinz, and Lammers, Konrad. 1979. "Subventionen in der Bundesrepublik Deutschland." In *Kiel Discussion Papers*, no. 63/64. Kiel: Institut für Welt Wirtschaft.

Kaplan, Robert. 1979. "An Optimal Indexing Method for Social Security." In *Financing Social Security*, ed. Colin D. Campbell. Washington, D.C.: American Enterprise Institute.

Kurz, Mordecai, and Arvin, Marcy. 1979. "Social Security and Capital Formation: The Funding Controversy." Paper prepared for the President's Commission on Pension Policy (September). Washington, D.C.

Leimer, D., and Lesnoy, S. 1980. "Social Security and Private Saving: A Reexamination of the Time-Series Evidence Using Alternative Social Security Wealth Variables." Mimeographed.

Logue, D. E. 1979. "How Social Security May Undermine the Private Industrial Pension System." In *Financing Social Security*, ed. Colin D. Campbell. Washington, D.C.: American Enterprise Institute.

Löwe, Horst. 1978. "Demographisch bedingte Probleme der Versorgung alter Menschen." In *Konsequenzen des Geburtenrückgangs für ausgewählte Politikbereiche*. Stuttgart, Federal Republic of Germany.

Mackenroth, Gerhard. 1957. "Die Reform der Sozialpolitik durch einen deutschen Sozialplan." In *Sozialpolitik und Sozialreform*, ed. Erik Boettcher. Tübingen, Federal Republic of Germany.

Meinhold, Helmut. 1978. "Ökonomische Probleme der Sozialen Sicherheit." *Kieler Vorträge*, N.F. 86. Tübingen, Federal Republic of Germany: Mohr.

Mishan, E. J. 1969. In *Public Finance*, ed. C. S. Shoup. Hawthorne, NY: Aldine Publishing Co.

Müller, Stefan. 1978. *Entstehung und Entwicklung der AHV von 1945-1978*. Fribourg, Switzerland: University of Fribourg.

Munnell, A. 1974. *The Effect of Social Security on Personal Savings*. Cambridge, MA: Ballinger.

_____. 1979. "The Future of the U.S. Pension System." In *Financing Social Security*, ed. Colin D. Campbell. Washington, D.C.: American Enterprise Institute.

Musgrave, R. A. 1959. *The Theory of Public Finance*. New York: McGraw-Hill.

Nell-Breuning, Oswald v. 1980. "Soziale Rentenversicherung in familien- und bevölkerungspolitischer Sicht." *Die neue ordnung* 34 (Bonn).

Oberhänsli, Urs. 1981. "Einfluss der AHV und der beruflichen Vorsorge auf die persönlichen Ersparnisse in der Schweiz." Ph.D. dissertation, University of Zurich, Switzerland.

O'Neill, J. A. 1979. "Alternatives for Financing a Mature Social Security System." In *Financing Social Security*, ed. Colin D. Campbell. Washington, D.C.: American Enterprise Institute.

Patton, Carl V. 1977. "The Politics of Social Security." In *The Crisis of Social Security*, ed. Michael J. Boskin. San Francisco, CA: Institute for Contemporary Studies.

Petersen, Hans-Georg. 1979. "Finanzwirtschaftliche Folgen einer Harmonisierung der Belastung von Arbeits- und Alterseinkommen mit öffentlichen Abgaben." In *Kiel Working Papers*, no. 93.

_____. 1981*a*. "Impact of the Tax System—The Case of the Federal Republic of Germany." In *The International Impact of Taxation*, ed. Michael Walker. Vancouver, BC: The Fraser Institute.

_____. 1981*b*. *Sicherheit der Renten? Die Zukunft der Altersversorgung*. Würzburg, Wien: Physica-Verlag.

_____. 1981*c*. "Taxes, Tax Systems and Economic Growth." In *Towards Explaining Economic Growth*, ed. Herbert Giersch. Tübingen, Federal Republic of Germany.

Picot, Michel. 1980. "Effets des régimes obligatoires de retraite sur l'offre d'épargne des ménages." Doctoral thesis, Université d'Orléans, France.

Rosen, Sherwin. 1977. "Social Security and the Economy." In *The Crisis in Social Security*, ed. Michael J. Boskin. San Francisco, CA: Institute for Contemporary Studies.

Rosenberg, Peter. 1979. "Die Zukunft der Alterssicherung in der Bundesrepublik Deutschland." *Allgemeines Statistisches Archiv*, Göttingen (Federal Republic of Germany), vol. 63.

Rosse, J. N., and Panzar, J. C. 1977. "Chamberlin versus Robinson: An Empirical Test for Monopoly Rents." Studies in Industry Economics Discussion Paper, Department of Economics, Stanford University, Stanford, California.

Samuelson, P. A. 1969. In *Public Finance*, ed. C. S. Shoup. Hawthorne, NY: Aldine Publishing Co.

Schmidt-Kaler, Theodor. 1980. "Kinder statt Beiträge—Anregungen zu einer Rentenversicherung mit Selbstbeteiligung." *Die politische Meinung* 25 (Bonn).

_____. 1979. "Wie sicher sind unsere Renten?" *Aus Politik und Zeitgeschichte* 27 (Bonn).

Schweizer, Willy. 1980. *Die wirtschaftliche Lage der Rentner in der Schweiz.* Bern and Stuttgart: Paul Haupt.

Shoup, C. S. 1969. *Public Finance.* Hawthorne, NY: Aldine Publishing Company.

Switzerland. (Various years.) *Statistisches Jahrbuch der Schweiz.* Bern, Switzerland: Bundesamt für Statistik.

_____. (Various years.) *Die Volkswirtschaft.* Bern, Switzerland: Eidgenössisches Volkswirtschaftsdepartement.

Transfer-Enquête-Kommission. 1979. *Zur Einkommenslage der Rentner. Zwischenbericht der Kommission.* Bonn: Veröffentlicht durch die Bundesregierung.

U.S. Department of Health, Education, and Welfare. 1979. *Work, Income and Retirement of the Aged.* Technical Analysis Paper 18, Office of Income Security. Washington, D.C.: HEW.

Valiani, R. 1969. "Le alternative di finanziamento della sicurezza sociale." *Rivista internazionale di scienze sociali* 1.

von Furstenberg, G. M., ed. 1979. *Social Security versus Private Saving in Post-Industrial Democracies.* Cambridge, MA: Ballinger.

Walker, Michael, ed. 1981. *The International Impact of Taxation.* Vancouver, British Columbia.

Witte, Edwin. 1962. *The Development of the Social Security Act.* Madison, WI: University of Wisconsin Press.

Zabalza, A.; Pissarides, E.; and Barton, M. 1980*a*. "Social Security and the Choice between Full-Time Work, Part-Time Work and Retirement." *Journal of Public Economics* 14.

Zabalza, A.; Pissarides, C. A.; and Piachaud, D. 1980*b*. "Social Security, Life-Cycle Savings and Retirement." In *The Limits to Redistribution*, ed. D. A. Collard, J. R. Lecomber, and M. D. E. Slater. London: John Wright and Sons.

Zeppernick, Ralf. 1979. "Kritische Bemerkungen zum Zusammenhang zwischen Alterslastenausgleich und Kinderlastenausgleich." *Finanzarchiv, N.F.* 37.

ABOUT THE AUTHORS

ONORATO CASTELLINO is professor of economics, teaching economic principles, in the Istituto di Economia Politica at the University of Turin, Italy. His research on monetary and credit policy led him to study the economics of social security and to publication of his book, *Il labirinto delle pensioni* (The Labyrinth of Pensions) in 1976. He has also written a number of journal articles, along with reports for departments in the Italian government.

A. LAWRENCE CHICKERING is a founder and currently executive director of the Institute for Contemporary Studies, a public policy research institute based in San Francisco. Besides editing more than twenty-five books on a wide range of policy issues for the Institute, he is also editor of the *Journal of Contemporary Studies*, the Institute's quarterly public policy journal.

RICHARD HEMMING is senior research officer in the Institute for Fiscal Studies, London. He is the author of a number of articles on the economics of retirement systems and taxation policy published in British, Scottish, Australian, and European journals and, with John A. Kay, of *Value Added Tax: The UK Experience* to be published by The Brookings Institution, Washington, D.C.

MARTIN C. JANSSEN is senior research fellow and lecturer in economics at the University of Zurich, Switzerland. His post-doctoral studies in economics and finance at the University of Rochester, New York, were financed by the Swiss National Science Foundation. He is the author of articles on economics and finance, and of two books—*A Monetary Model for Small Open Economies: Structure and Dynamic Characteristics* and, with K. Hummler, *An Economico-Legal Analysis of the Proposal to Alter the Swiss Federal Constitution.*

KARL HEINZ JÜTTEMEIER is research fellow for the study program in public finance at the Kiel Institute of World Economics in West Germany. His studies of West Germany's economic problems include theoretical and empirical analyses of budgetary stabilization policies as well as the allocational impacts of subsidy programs.

JOHN A. KAY, research director for the Institute for Fiscal Studies, London, is special advisor to the House of Commons Select Committee on the Treasury and Civil Service Departments. He is the author and coauthor of numerous articles on taxation and economic problems published in British and French journals, and his books include *Concentration in Modern Industry*, written with L. Hannah, and *The British Tax System*, coauthored with M. A. King.

233

HEINZ H. MÜLLER is research associate in the Institute for Empirical Research in Economics at the University of Zürich, Switzerland. His research in mathematical economics and problems of social security included studies at the University of California, Berkeley, in the application of mathematics and statistics to economics, a year at the Center for Operations Research and Econometrics at the Catholic University of Louvain, Belgium, and later studies in the Faculty of Economics and Politics, University of Cambridge, England. His publications have appeared in economic journals.

HANS-GEORG PETERSEN, professor of political science, is a lecturer in public finance at the University of Kiel, West Germany. A former member of the research staff at the Kiel Institute of World Economics, his articles on public finance and social policy are published widely in international economic journals. His books include *Personnelle Einkommensbesteuerung und Inflation* (Personal Income Taxation and Inflation) and *Sicherheit der Altersversorgung* (Security for Pensions).

JEAN-JACQUES ROSA, professor of economics at the Institut d'Etudes Politiques de Paris, is founder of the Fondation Nationale d'Economie Politique, concerned with economic problems of the French social security system, unemployment, government regulation, and government-created monopolies. He is the author of numerous articles on economic and political subjects published in international journals, and his most recent books include *La Répression Financière* (The Policy of Financial Repression) and, forthcoming, *The Economics of Labor Unions.*

SHERWIN ROSEN is professor of economics at the University of Chicago and research associate at the National Opinion Research Center. He is associate editor of *Econometrica* and *Economics Letters*, and the author of many articles on economic aspects of social policies. His chapter on "Social Security and the Economy" appeared in *The Crisis in Social Security*, published by the Institute for Contemporary Studies in 1977.

INGEMAR STÅHL, professor of economics at Lund University in Sweden, is a former consultant and adviser to the Swedish ministries of education and finance and head of the Planning Programming Budgeting System at the Swedish ministry of defense. In 1970 he spent a year in Paris dealing with labor and social questions at the Organization of Economic Cooperation and Development. Social and health economics and the government redistribution programs receive his attention at present, and his principle publications are concerned with housing and industrial policies.

NORIYUKI TAKAYAMA is associate professor of economics at Hitotsubashi University, Tokyo, Japan. He is the author of *Redistribution Policies in Postwar Japan: Theory and Practice*, and of "Poverty, Income Inequality, and Their Measures: Professor Sen's Axiomatic Approach Reconsidered," published in *Econometrica*.

INDEX

PUBLICATIONS LIST*
THE INSTITUTE FOR CONTEMPORARY STUDIES
260 California Street, San Francisco, California 94111
Catalog available upon request

BUREAUCRATS AND BRAINPOWER: GOVERNMENT
REGULATION OF UNIVERSITIES
$6.95. 170 pages. Publication date: June 1979
ISBN 0—917616—35—9
Library of Congress No. 79—51328
Contributors: Nathan Glazer, Robert S. Hatfield, Richard
W. Lyman, Paul Seabury, Robert L. Sproull, Miro
M. Todorovich, Caspar W. Weinberger

THE CALIFORNIA COASTAL PLAN: A CRITIQUE
$5.95. 199 pages. Publication date: March 1976
ISBN 0—917616—04—9
Library of Congress No. 76—7715
Contributors: Eugene Bardach, Daniel K. Benjamin, Thomas E.
Borcherding, Ross D. Eckert, H. Edward Frech III,
M. Bruce Johnson, Ronald N. Lafferty, Walter J. Mead,
Daniel Orr, Donald M. Pach, Michael R. Peevey

THE CRISIS IN SOCIAL SECURITY: PROBLEMS AND
PROSPECTS
$6.95. 222 pages. Publication date: April 1977; 2d rev., 1978,
1979
ISBN 0—917616—16—2/1977; 0—917616—25—1/1978
Library of Congress No. 77—72542
Contributors: Michael J. Boskin, George F. Break, Rita Ricardo
Campbell, Edward Cowan, Martin S. Feldstein, Milton
Friedman, Douglas R. Munro, Donald O. Parsons, Carl
V. Patton, Joseph A. Pechman, Sherwin Rosen, W. Kip
Viscusi, Richard J. Zeckhauser

THE ECONOMY IN THE 1980s: A PROGRAM FOR GROWTH
AND STABILITY
$7.95 (paper). 462 pages. Publication date: June 1980
ISBN 0—917616—39—1
Library of Congress No. 80—80647
$17.95 (cloth). 462 pages. Publication date : August 1980
ISBN 0—87855—399—1. Available through Transaction

* Prices subject to change.

Books, Rutgers—The State University, New Brunswick,
NJ 08903
Contributors: Michael J. Boskin, George F. Break, John
T. Cuddington, Patricia Drury, Alain Enthoven, Laurence
J. Kotlikoff, Ronald I. McKinnon, John H. Pencavel, Henry
S. Rowen, John L. Scadding, John B. Shoven, James
L. Sweeney, David J. Teece

EMERGING COALITIONS IN AMERICAN POLITICS
$6.95. 524 pages. Publication date: June 1978
ISBN 0—917616—22—7
Library of Congress No. 78—53414
Contributors: Jack Bass, David S. Broder, Jerome M. Clubb,
Edward H. Crane III, Walter De Vries, Andrew M. Greeley,
S. I. Hayakawa, Tom Hayden, Milton Himmelfarb, Richard
Jensen, Paul Kleppner, Everett Carll Ladd, Jr., Seymour
Martin Lipset, Robert A. Nisbet, Michael Novak, Gary
R. Orren, Nelson W. Polsby, Joseph L. Rauh, Jr., Stanley
Rothman, William A. Rusher, William Schneider, Jesse
M. Unruh, Ben J. Wattenberg

THE FAIRMONT PAPERS: BLACK ALTERNATIVES
CONFERENCE, SAN FRANCISCO, DECEMBER 1980
$5.95. 174 pages. Publication date: March 1981
ISBN 0—917616—42—1
Library of Congress No. 81—80735
Contributors: Bernard E. Anderson, Thomas L. Berkley, Michael
J. Boskin, Randolph W. Bromery, Tony Brown, Milton
Friedman, Wendell Wilkie Gunn, Charles V. Hamilton,
Robert B. Hawkins, Jr., Maria Lucia Johnson, Martin
L. Kilson, James Lorenz, Henry Lucas, Jr., Edwin Meese
III, Clarence M. Pendleton, Jr., Dan J. Smith, Thomas
Sowell, Chuck Stone, Percy E. Sutton, Clarence Thomas,
Gloria E. A. Toote, Walter E. Williams, Oscar Wright

FEDERAL TAX REFORM: MYTHS AND REALITIES
$5.95. 270 pages. Publication date: September 1978
ISBN 0—917616—32—4
Library of Congress No. 78—61661
Contributors: Robert J. Barro, Michael J. Boskin, George
F. Break, Jerry R. Green, Laurence J. Kotlikoff, Mordecai
Kurz, Peter Mieszkowski, John B. Shoven, Paul J.
Taubman, John Whalley

GOVERNMENT CREDIT ALLOCATION: WHERE DO WE GO
FROM HERE?
$4.95. 208 pages. Publication date: November 1975
ISBN 0—917616—02—2
Library of Congress No. 75—32951
Contributors: George J. Benston, Karl Brunner, Dwight M. Jaffe,
Omotunde E. G. Johnson, Edward J. Kane, Thomas Mayer,
Allan H. Meltzer

NATIONAL SECURITY IN THE 1980s: FROM WEAKNESS TO
STRENGTH
$8.95 (paper). 524 pages. Publication date: May 1980
ISBN 0—917616—38—3
Library of Congress No. 80—80648
$19.95 (cloth). 524 pages. Publication date: August 1980
ISBN 0—87855—412—2. Available through Transaction
Books, Rutgers—The State University, New Brunswick,
NJ 08903
Contributors: Kenneth L. Adelman, Richard R. Burt, Miles M.
Costick, Robert F. Ellsworth, Fred Charles Ikl'e, Geoffrey
T. H. Kemp, Edward N. Luttwak, Charles Burton Marshall,
Paul H. Nitze, Sam Nunn, Henry S. Rowen, Leonard
Sullivan, Jr., W. Scott Thompson, William R. Van Cleave,
Francis J. West, Jr., Albert Wohlstetter, Elmo R. Zumwalt,
Jr.

NEW DIRECTIONS IN PUBLIC HEALTH CARE:
A PRESCRIPTION FOR THE 1980s
$6.95 (paper). 279 pages. Publication date: May 1976;
3d ed. rev., 1980
ISBN 0—917616—37—5
Library of Congress No. 79—92868
$16.95 (cloth). 290 pages. Publication date: April 1980
ISBN 0—87855—394—0. Available through Transaction
Books, Rutgers—The State University, New Brunswick,
NJ 08903
Contributors: Alain Enthoven, W. Philip Gramm, Leon R. Kass,
Keith B. Leffler, Cotton M. Lindsay, Jack A. Meyer, Charles
E. Phelps, Thomas C. Schelling, Harry Schwartz, Arthur
Seldon, David A. Stockman, Lewis Thomas

OPTIONS FOR U.S. ENERGY POLICY
$6.95. 317 pages. Publication date: September 1977
ISBN 0—917616—20—0

Library of Congress No. 77—89094

Contributors: Albert Carnesale, Stanley M. Greenfield, Fred S. Hoffman, Edward J. Mitchell, William R. Moffat, Richard Nehring, Robert S. Pindyck, Norman C. Rasmussen, David J. Rose, Henry S. Rowen, James L. Sweeney, Arthur W. Wright

PARENTS, TEACHERS, AND CHILDREN: PROSPECTS FOR CHOICE IN AMERICAN EDUCATION

$5.95. 336 pages. Publication date: June 1977
ISBN 0—917616—18—9
Library of Congress No. 77—79164

Contributors: James S. Coleman, John E. Coons, William H. Cornog, Denis P. Doyle, E. Babette Edwards, Nathan Glazer, Andrew M. Greeley, R. Kent Greenawalt, Marvin Lazerson, William C. McCready, Michael Novak, John P. O'Dwyer, Robert Singleton, Thomas Sowell, Stephen D. Sugarman, Richard E. Wagner

PARTY COALITIONS IN THE 1980s

$8.95 (paper). 480 pages. Publication date: November 1981
ISBN 0—917616—43—X
Library of Congress No. 81—83095
$19.95 (cloth). 480 pages. Publication date: November 1981
ISBN 0—917616—45—6

Contributors: John B. Anderson, David S. Broder, Walter Dean Brunham, Patrick Caddell, Jerome M. Clubb, E. J. Dionne, Jr., Alan M. Fisher, Michael Harrington, S. I. Hayakawa, Richard Jensen, Paul Kleppner, Everett Carll Ladd, Seymour Martin Lipset, Arthur D. Miller, Howard Phillips, Norman Podhoretz, Nelson W. Polsby, Richard M. Scammon, William Schneider, Martin P. Wattenberg, Richard B. Wirthlin.

POLITICS AND THE OVAL OFFICE: TOWARDS PRESIDENTIAL GOVERNANCE

$7.95 (paper). 332 pages. Publication date: February 1981
ISBN 0—917616—40—5
Library of Congress No. 80—69617
$18.95 (cloth). 300 pages. Publication date: April 1981
ISBN 0—87855—428—9. Available through Transaction Books, Rutgers—The State University, New Brunswick, NJ 08903

Contributors: Richard K. Betts, Jack Citrin, Eric L. Davis, Robert
    M. Entman, Robert E. Hall, Hugh Heclo, Everett Carll
    Ladd, Jr., Arnold J. Meltsner, Charles Peters, Robert
    S. Pindyck, Francis E. Rourke, Martin M. Shapiro, Peter
    L. Szanton

THE POLITICS OF PLANNING: A REVIEW AND CRITIQUE
OF CENTRALIZED ECONOMIC PLANNING
    $5.95. 367 pages. Publication date: March 1976
    ISBN 0—917616—05—7
    Library of Congress No. 76—7714
Contributors: B. Bruce-Briggs, James Buchanan, A. Lawrence
    Chickering, Ralph Harris, Robert B. Hawkins, Jr., George
    W. Hilton, Richard Mancke, Richard Muth, Vincent Ostrom,
    Svetozar Pejovich, Myron Sharpe, John Sheahan, Herbert
    Stein, Gordon Tullock, Ernest van den Haag, Paul
    H. Weaver, Murray L. Weidenbaum, Hans Willgerodt, Peter
    P. Witonski

PUBLIC EMPLOYEE UNIONS: A STUDY OF THE CRISIS IN
PUBLIC SECTOR LABOR RELATIONS
    $6.95. 251 pages. Publication date: June 1976; 2d rev., 1977
    ISBN 0—917616—24—3
    Library of Congress No. 76—18409
Contributors: A. Lawrence Chickering, Jack D. Douglas, Raymond
    D. Horton, Theodore W. Kheel, David Lewin, Seymour
    Martin Lipset, Harvey C. Mansfield, Jr., George Meany,
    Robert A. Nisbet, Daniel Orr, A. H. Raskin, Wes Uhlman,
    Harry H. Wellington, Charles B. Wheeler, Jr., Ralph
    K. Winter, Jr., Jerry Wurf

REGULATING BUSINESS: THE SEARCH FOR AN OPTIMUM
    $6.95. 261 pages. Publication date: April 1978
    ISBN 0—917616—27—8
    Library of Congress No. 78—50678
Contributors: Chris Argyris, A. Lawrence Chickering, Penny
    Hollander Feldman, Richard H. Holton, Donald P. Jacobs,
    Alfred E. Kahn, Paul W. MacAvoy, Almarin Phillips,
    V. Kerry Smith, Paul H. Weaver, Richard J. Zeckhauser

SOCIAL REGULATION: STRATEGIES FOR REFORM
    $8.95 (paper). 420 pages. Publication date: March 1982
    ISBN 0—917616—46—4
    Library of Congress No. 81—85279

$19.95 (cloth). 420 pages. Publication date: March 1982
ISBN 0—87855—47—2

Contributors: Lawrence S. Bacow, Eugene Bardach, Paul
    Danaceau, George C. Eads, Joseph Ferreira, Jr., Thomas
    P. Grumbly, William R. Havender, Robert A. Kagan,
    Michael H. Levin, Michael O'Hare, Stuart M. Pape,
    Timothy J. Sullivan

TARIFFS, QUOTAS, AND TRADE: THE POLITICS OF
PROTECTIONISM
$7.95. 332 pages. Publication date: February 1979
ISBN 0—917616—34—0
Library of Congress No. 78—66267

Contributors: Walter Adams, Ryan C. Amacher, Sven W. Arndt,
    Malcolm D. Bale, John T. Cuddington, Alan V. Deardorff,
    Joel B. Dirlam, Roger D. Hansen, H. Robert Heller, D. Gale
    Johnson, Robert O. Keohane, Michael W. Keran, Rachel
    McCulloch, Ronald I. McKinnon, Gordon W. Smith, Robert
    M. Stern, Richard James Sweeney, Robert D. Tollison,
    Thomas D. Willett

THE THIRD WORLD: PREMISES OF U.S. POLICY
$7.95. 334 pages. Publication date: November 1978
ISBN 0—917616—30—8
Library of Congress No. 78—67593

Contributors: Dennis Austin, Peter T. Bauer, Max Beloff, Richard
    E. Bissell, Daniel J. Elazar, S. E. Finer, Allan E. Goodman,
    Nathaniel H. Leff, Seymour Martin Lipset, Edward
    N. Luttwak, Daniel Pipes, Wilson E. Schmidt, Anthony
    Smith, W. Scott Thompson, Basil S. Yamey

UNION CONTROL OF PENSION FUNDS: WILL THE NORTH
RISE AGAIN?
$2.00. 41 pages. Publication date: July 1979
ISBN 0—917616—36—7
Library of Congress No. 78—66581

Author: George J. Borjas

WATER BANKING: HOW TO STOP WASTING
AGRICULTURAL WATER
$2.00. 56 pages. Publication date: January 1978
ISBN 0—917616—26—X
Library of Congress No. 78—50766

Authors: Sotirios Angelides, Eugene Bardach

WHAT'S NEWS: THE MEDIA IN AMERICAN SOCIETY

$7.95 (paper). 296 pages. Publication date: June 1981
ISBN 0—917616—41—3
Library of Congress No. 81—81414
$18.95 (cloth). 300 pages. Publication date: August 1981
ISBN 0—87855—448—3. Available through Transaction
Books, Rutgers—The State University, New Brunswick,
NJ 08903

Contributors: Elie Abel, Robert L. Bartley, George Comstock,
Edward Jay Epstein, William A. Henry III, John L. Hulteng,
Theodore Peterson, Ithiel de Sola Pool, William E. Porter,
Michael Jay Robinson, James N. Rosse, Benno C. Schmidt,
Jr.

THE WORLD CRISIS IN SOCIAL SECURITY

$9.95 260 pages. Publication date : April 1982
ISBN 0—917616—44—8

Contributors: Onorato Castellino, A. Lawrence Chickering, Richard
Hemming, Martin C. Janssen, Karl Heinz Jüttemeier, John
A. Kay, Heinz H. Müller, Hans-Georg Petersen, Jean-
Jacques Rosa, Sherwin Rosen, Ingemar Ståhl, Noriyuki
Takayama

JOURNAL OF CONTEMPORARY STUDIES

$15/one year, $25/two years, $4/single issue. For delivery
outside the United States, add $2/year surface mail,
$10/year airmail

A quarterly journal that is a forum for lively and readable studies on
foreign and domestic public policy issues. Directed toward
general readers as well as policymakers and academics,
emphasizing debate and controversy, it publishes the highest
quality articles without regard to political or ideological bent.

The Journal of Contemporary Studies is a member of the
Transaction Periodicals Consortium. Institute for Contemporary
Studies books are distributed by Transaction Books, Rutgers
University, New Brunswick, NJ 08903.

Imprimerie Bayeusaine, 8-12, rue Royale, 14401 Bayeux
Dépôt légal : avril 1982
N° d'Imprimeur : 4792 - N° de chemise : 4290
Imprimé en France le 16 avril 1982